First World War
and Army of Occupation
War Diary
France, Belgium and Germany

29 DIVISION
87 Infantry Brigade,
Brigade Machine Gun Company
2 June 1916 - 28 January 1918

WO95/2305/6

The Naval & Military Press Ltd
www.nmarchive.com
Published in association with The National Archives

Published by

The Naval & Military Press Ltd

Unit 10 Ridgewood Industrial Park,

Uckfield, East Sussex,

TN22 5QE England

Tel: +44 (0) 1825 749494

www.naval-military-press.com

www.nmarchive.com

This diary has been reprinted in facsimile from the original. Any imperfections are inevitably reproduced and the quality may fall short of modern type and cartographic standards.

© **Crown Copyright**
Images reproduced by permission of The National Archives, London, England, 2015.

Contents

Document type	Place/Title	Date From	Date To
Heading	WO95/2305-6 87 Brigade Machine Gun Company. June'16-Jan'18		
Heading	29th Division 87th Infy Bde 87th Mach. Gun Coy. Jun 1916-Jan 1918		
Heading	29th Division 87th Infantry Brigade. 87th Machine Gun Company June 1916 Appendices attached-Operation Orders Nominal Rolls.		
Heading	War Diary Of 87th M.G. Coy. From June 1st 1916. To June 30th 1916. Volume I.		
War Diary	Englebelmer	02/06/1916	14/06/1916
War Diary	Louvencourt	15/06/1916	23/06/1916
War Diary	Englebelmer	26/06/1916	30/06/1916
Miscellaneous	Appendix I N.C.O. & Men Of The 87th Bde Machine Gun Coy Transferred To The M.G. Corps:-		
Operation(al) Order(s)	Operation Order No.1 By Capt H.R. Burrell Commdg. 87th Bde Machine Gun Coy Appendix	19/06/1916	19/06/1916
Miscellaneous	Headquarters 87th Bde. M.G. Coy.		
Operation(al) Order(s)	Index To Copies Of Operation Order No.2. Appendix 3	21/06/1916	21/06/1916
Operation(al) Order(s)	Operation Order No.2. By Capt. H.R. Burrell, Comdg. 87th Bde. Machine Gun Coy.		
Miscellaneous Miscellaneous	Certificate To Be Signed before Fire is Opened.		
Miscellaneous Miscellaneous	Certificate To Be Signed before Fire is Opened.		
Miscellaneous Miscellaneous	Certificate To Be Signed before Fire is Opened.		
Miscellaneous Miscellaneous	Certificate To Be Signed before Fire is Opened.		
Miscellaneous	Certificate To Be Signed before Fire is Opened.		
Operation(al) Order(s)	Operation Order No.3. by capt H.R. Burrell, Comdg. 87th Bde Machine Gun Coy. Appendix 4	23/06/1916	23/06/1916
Map	Beaumont Hamel. Appendix 5		
Operation(al) Order(s)	87th Bde Machine Gun Coy. Operation Order No.4. Appendix 6	25/06/1916	25/06/1916
Operation(al) Order(s)	87th Bde Machine Gun Company Operation Order No.5. Appendix 7	29/06/1916	29/06/1916
Heading	29th Division, 87th Infantry Brigade. 87th Machine Gun Company July 1916 Appendices attached:- Operation Orders. Special Orders of the Day		
Heading	War Diary Of 87th M.G.Coy. From July 1st 1916 To July 31st 1916. Volume II.		
War Diary	Englebelmer Sector	01/07/1916	08/07/1916
War Diary	Englebelmer	09/07/1916	24/07/1916
War Diary	Bus	25/07/1916	25/07/1916
War Diary	Amplier.	26/07/1916	27/07/1916
War Diary	Proven	30/07/1916	31/07/1916
Miscellaneous	List Of Casualties In Action On July 1st 1916 87th Bde Machine Gun Company. Appendix I	01/07/1916	01/07/1916

Type	Description	Date From	Date To
Miscellaneous	Message. From Lieut.-General Sir Aylmer Hunter-Weston K.C.B. D.S.O. To All Officers. N.C.O's And Men Of The VIII. Army Corps. Appendix 2	04/07/1916	04/07/1916
Miscellaneous	Special Order Of The Day By General Sir Douglas Haig, G.C.B., K.C.I.E., K.C.V.O., A.D.C. Commander-In-Chief, British Armies In France. Appendix 3.	18/07/1916	18/07/1916
Miscellaneous	87th Brigade Machine Gun Coy Operations Order No 6	26/07/1916	26/07/1916
Miscellaneous	Train Line Table		
Miscellaneous	Special Order Of The Day By General Sir Douglas Haig, G.C.B., K.C.I.E., K.C.V.O., A.D.C. Commander-In-Chief, British Armies In France. Appendix 5.	27/07/1916	27/07/1916
Heading	29th Division. 87th Infantry Brigade. 87th Machine Gun Company August 1916		
Heading	War Diary Of 87th Machine Gun Company From August 1st 1916 To August 31st 1916 (Volume)		
War Diary	Ypres	02/08/1916	08/08/1916
War Diary	Brandhoek	09/08/1916	18/08/1916
War Diary	Ypres	19/08/1916	31/08/1916
Heading	29th Division. 87th Infantry Brigade. 87th Machine Gun Company September 1916		
Heading	War Diary Of 87th Machine Gun Company From September 1st To September 30th 1916 (Volume 4		
War Diary	Ypres	01/09/1916	08/09/1916
War Diary	Brandhoek	11/09/1916	16/09/1916
War Diary	Ypres	18/09/1916	30/09/1916
Miscellaneous	Appendix I		
Miscellaneous	Appendix II		
Operation(al) Order(s)	87th Machine Gun Company Operation Order No 8 Appendix III	30/09/1916	30/09/1916
Map			
Heading	29th Division, 87th Infantry Brigade. 87th Machine Gun Company October 1916.		
Heading	War Diary Of 87th Machine Gun Company From October 1st 1916 To October 31st 1916. (Volume 5)		
War Diary	Ypres	03/10/1916	03/10/1916
War Diary	'J' Camp	07/10/1916	07/10/1916
War Diary	Allonville	08/10/1916	10/10/1916
War Diary	Buire	14/10/1916	14/10/1916
War Diary	Fricourt	18/10/1916	19/10/1916
War Diary	Bernafay	20/10/1916	20/10/1916
War Diary	Trenches	21/10/1916	30/10/1916
War Diary	Fricourt	31/10/1916	31/10/1916
Operation(al) Order(s)	87th Machine Gun Company. Operation Order No.9.	20/10/1916	20/10/1916
Operation(al) Order(s)	87th Machine Gun Company. Operation Order No 9 Appendix II	23/10/1916	23/10/1916
Operation(al) Order(s)	87th Machine Gun Company Operation Order No.11. Appendix III		
Heading	29th Division. 87th Infantry Brigade. 87th Machine Gun Company November 1916		
Heading	War Diary Of 87th Machine Gun Company From 1st November 1916 To 30th November 1916. (Volume 6.)		
War Diary	Fricourt	01/11/1916	03/11/1916
War Diary	Airaines	07/11/1916	12/11/1916
War Diary	Citadel	14/11/1916	14/11/1916
War Diary	Bricqueterie	15/11/1916	15/11/1916
War Diary	Guillemont	16/11/1916	24/11/1916

Type	Location/Description	From	To
War Diary	Carnoy	25/11/1916	25/11/1916
Heading	29th Division. 87th Infantry Brigade 87th Machine Gun Company December 1916		
Heading	War Diary Of 87th Machine Gun Company. From. 1st December 1916 To 31st December 1916. (Volume 7.)		
War Diary	Carnoy	01/12/1916	03/12/1916
War Diary	Lesboeufs	05/12/1916	11/12/1916
War Diary	Citadel	12/12/1916	12/12/1916
War Diary	Mericourt	13/12/1916	13/12/1916
War Diary	Soues	18/12/1916	30/12/1916
Heading	War Diary Of 87th Machine Gun Company. From January 1st 1917 To January 31st 1917. Volume 8		
War Diary	In The Field	01/01/1917	31/01/1917
Operation(al) Order(s)	87th Machine Gun Company. Operation Order No 14	25/01/1917	25/01/1917
Map			
Miscellaneous	Report On Machine Gun Operation On The 27th Inst	29/01/1917	29/01/1917
Heading	War Diary Of 87th Machine Gun Company. From 1st February 1917 To 28th February.1917. (Volume 9)		
War Diary	In The Field	05/02/1917	28/02/1917
Operation(al) Order(s)	87th Machine Gun Company Operation Order No.15.	25/02/1917	25/02/1917
Heading	War Diary Of 87th Machine Gun Company From 1st March 1917 To 31st March 1917. (Volume 10)		
War Diary	Combles	03/03/1917	03/03/1917
War Diary	Bronfay	04/03/1917	04/03/1917
War Diary	Bussy	05/03/1917	19/03/1917
War Diary	Soues	24/03/1917	29/03/1917
War Diary	Vignacourt	30/03/1917	30/03/1917
Heading	War Diary Of 87th Machine Gun Company For 1st April 1917 To 30th April 1917. (Volume II)		
War Diary	Fieffes	01/04/1917	01/04/1917
War Diary	Hem	02/04/1917	02/04/1917
War Diary	Lucheux	03/04/1917	05/04/1917
War Diary	Etree-Wamin	07/04/1917	07/04/1917
War Diary	Warluzel	08/04/1917	08/04/1917
War Diary	Bavincourt	11/04/1917	12/04/1917
War Diary	Feuchy	14/04/1917	14/04/1917
War Diary	Guemappe Sector	15/04/1917	19/04/1917
War Diary	Arras	21/04/1917	22/04/1917
War Diary	Monchy.	23/04/1917	24/04/1917
War Diary	Arras	25/04/1917	25/04/1917
War Diary	Duisans	26/04/1917	26/04/1917
War Diary	Habarcq	27/04/1917	27/04/1917
War Diary	Laherliere	30/04/1917	30/04/1917
Operation(al) Order(s)	87th Machine Gun Company Operation Order No.16 Appendix I	21/04/1917	21/04/1917
Miscellaneous	H.Q 87th Infantry Brigade. Appendix. 2		
Miscellaneous	At 1600. By No.3 Sector.		
Miscellaneous	O.C. No 3 Section REAM.	26/04/1917	26/04/1917
Miscellaneous	29th Division Instructions No.3.	20/04/1917	20/04/1917
Miscellaneous	87th Machine Gun Company.		
Heading	War Diary Of 87th Machine Gun Company. From 1st May 1917 To 31st May 1917 Volume XII		
War Diary	In The Field	01/05/1917	31/05/1917
Operation(al) Order(s)	87th Machine Gun Company Operation Order No.16. Appendix I	18/05/1917	18/05/1917
Operation(al) Order(s)	87th Machine Gun Company Operation Order No.16	18/05/1917	18/05/1917

Miscellaneous	NEALM		
Miscellaneous	War Diary Of 87th Machine Gun Company 1st June 1917 To 30th June 1917 (Volume 13)		
War Diary	In The Field	03/06/1917	28/06/1917
Miscellaneous	Third Army With Reference To Third Army Letter No. G26/93	27/03/1917	27/03/1917
Heading	War Diary Of 87th Machine Gun Company 1st July 1917 To 31st July 1917 (Volume XIV)		
War Diary	Nr Ypres	01/07/1917	08/07/1917
War Diary	Nr Crombeke	09/07/1917	23/07/1917
War Diary	Praed Camp	24/07/1917	30/07/1917
Operation(al) Order(s)	87th Machine Gun Company Operation Order (Preliminary) No 1	30/07/1917	30/07/1917
Heading	War Diary Of 87th Machine Gun Company From 1st August 1917 To 31st August 1917 Volume XV		
War Diary	In The Field	01/08/1917	29/08/1917
Heading	Appendix I		
Operation(al) Order(s)	87th Machine Gun Company Operation Order No. 18.	14/08/1917	14/08/1917
Operation(al) Order(s)	This Order To Be Attached To 87th Iny Coy Operation Order No.18		
Miscellaneous	Appendix II		
Heading	War Diary Of The 87th Machine Gun Company From 1st September 1917 To 30th September 1917. (Volume XVI)		
War Diary	In The Field	01/09/1917	30/09/1917
Heading	War Diary Of The 87th Machine Gun Company. From 1st October 1917 To 31st October 1917. (Volume XVII)		
War Diary	In The Field	02/10/1917	25/10/1917
Miscellaneous	War Diary. Of The 87th/29 Machine Gun Company From 1st November 1917 To 30th November 1917 (Volume XVIII)		
War Diary	Bellacourt	01/11/1917	17/11/1917
War Diary	Haut. Allaines	18/11/1917	18/11/1917
War Diary	Ains	19/11/1917	20/11/1917
War Diary	Marcoing	21/11/1917	30/11/1917
Miscellaneous	87th Machine Gun Company. Operation Order No.18. (Appendix I)	00/01/1917	00/11/1917
Heading	War Diary 87th Machine Gun Company. From 1st December 1917 To 31st December 1917. (Volume XIX)		
Heading	In The Line	01/12/1917	04/12/1917
War Diary	Sorel.	05/12/1917	05/12/1917
War Diary	Grand Rullecourt	07/12/1917	17/12/1917
War Diary	Vacquerie	18/12/1917	18/12/1917
War Diary	Wamin	19/12/1917	19/12/1917
War Diary	Henoville	20/12/1917	31/12/1917
Miscellaneous	Special Order Of The Day By Major General Sir Beauvoir De Lisle, K.C.B., D.S.O. Commanding 29th Division. (Appendix 1)	07/12/1917	07/12/1917
Heading	Special Order Of The Day By Major General Sir Beauvoir De Lisle, K.C.B., D.S.O. Commanding 29th Division.	07/12/1917	07/12/1917
Heading	War Diary Of The 87th Machine Gun Company. From 1st January 1918 To 31st January 1918. (Volume XX)		
War Diary	Henoville	03/01/1918	03/01/1918

War Diary	Borthes.	04/01/1918	04/01/1918
War Diary	La Val D'Acquin	05/01/1918	18/01/1918
War Diary	Vlamertinghe	20/01/1918	20/01/1918
War Diary	Brandhoek.	21/01/1918	28/01/1918

WO/95/2305/6

87 Brigade Machine Gun Company.

June '16 — Jan '18

29TH DIVISION
87TH INFY BDE

87TH MACH. GUN COY.
JUN 1916 - JAN 1918

29th Division

87th Infantry Brigade.

87th MACHINE GUN COMPANY

J U N E 1 9 1 6

Appendices attached - Operation Orders
Nominal Rolls.

CONFIDENTIAL

Vol I

War Diary
of
87th M.G. Coy.

From June 1st 1916. To June 30th 1916.

Volume I.

Army Form C. 2118.

WAR DIARY
or
INTELLIGENCE SUMMARY
(Erase heading not required.)

Instructions regarding War Diaries and Intelligence Summaries are contained in F. S. Regs., Part II. and the Staff Manual respectively. Title Pages will be prepared in manuscript.

Place	Date	Hour	Summary of Events and Information	Remarks and references to Appendices
ENGLEBELMER	June 2nd		No 3 Section relieved by No 1 Section, & proceeded to ENGLEBELMER.	
			Casualty. 1 man evacuated out of Divl Area 1/6, & struck off strength of Coy from that date.	
"	June 4th		One man admitted to Hospt in England on 23/5/16, & struck off strength of Coy from that date.	
"	June 6th		No 1 Section were relieved by No 3 Section, & proceeded to ENGLEBELMER.	
"	June 7th		7 men reported from 1st K.O.S.B., & taken on strength of Coy from this date.	
"	June 9th		1 Signaller reported from 1st Border Regt & taken on strength of Coy from this date.	
"	June 14th		87th M.G. Coy relieved by 86th M.G. Coy, & proceeded to LOUVENCOURT. The following detachments were attached and relieved as under from 16th June to 2nd July (inclusive)	
			2nd Lt Breene and 12 men to 2nd L.W.B.	
			Lt. CAYLEY and 12 men to 1st K.O.S.B.	
			Lt. COSTELLO and 12 men to 1st R. Innis. Fus.	
			2nd Lt. CRANFIELD and 12 men to 1st Border Regt.	
			All watches were altered from 2300 to 0000 at 2300	
LOUVENCOURT	June 15th		No 10046 1st Cpl. KERR reverted to P.te at his own request.	
	June 16th		1 man evacuated sick out of Divl Area on 14/6 & struck off strength of Coy from that date.	

Army Form C. 2118.

WAR DIARY
or
INTELLIGENCE SUMMARY
(Erase heading not required.)

Instructions regarding War Diaries and Intelligence Summaries are contained in F.S. Regs., Part II. and the Staff Manual respectively. Title Pages will be prepared in manuscript.

Place	Date	Hour	Summary of Events and Information	Remarks and references to Appendices
LOUVENCOURT	June 17th		The NCO's & men of 87th Bde M.G. Coy shewn in Appendix 1, were transferred to the Machine Gun Corps on the dates shewn. No 20957 Pte WORSLEY granted additional pay of 6d per day as Coy Cobbler from 6/6	See Appendix 2
"	June 18th		2nd Lt D.W. MEIN, 3rd S.W.B., to be 2nd in command 87th Bde M.G. Coy to fill establishment, dated 20th May 1916. 2nd Lt D.W. MEIN granted temporary rank of Capt whilst commanding 87th Bde M.G. Coy from Feb 1st 1916 — 19th May 1916. 87th Bde M.G. Coy Operation Order No 1 published.	
"	June 19th		2nd Lt MARSH with 1 gun, & 2nd Lt HUNTER with 1 gun, representing 2 complete sections took part in 29th Divl. Tactical Scheme. 87th Bde M.G. Coy Operation Order No 2 published. 87th Bde M.G. Coy Operation Order No 3 published.	See App. 3 See App. 4.
"	June 23rd		87th Bde M.G. Coy, less 8 guns, proceeded to ENGLEBELMER. The following proceeded to relieve 88th Bde M.G. Coy:— 3 Lt HUNTER with 2 guns occupied THURLES DUMP. 2nd Lt MARSH with 2 guns occupied SHOOTER'S HILL. 2nd Lt GREEN with 2 guns occupied OLD FIRING LINE & SAP 2. 2nd Lt FARRANT with 2 guns occupies F Street and D Street	See App. 5.

Army Form C. 2118.

WAR DIARY
or
INTELLIGENCE SUMMARY

(Erase heading not required.)

Instructions regarding War Diaries and Intelligence Summaries are contained in F. S. Regs., Part II. and the Staff Manual respectively. Title Pages will be prepared in manuscript.

Place	Date	Hour	Summary of Events and Information	Remarks and references to Appendices
ENGLEBELMER	June 26-27		Raid attempted on enemy trenches by NEWFOUNDLAND Regt. Guns of 87th M.G. Coy Co-operated. Operation Order No. 4 published	see App. 6.
"	June 29		"Z" day postponed 48 hours - Coy. Operation Order No 5 published	see App # 7
"	June 30		Coy. H.Q.rs moved up to FETHARD TRENCH, with 87th Bde H.Q.rs	

A.R. Burnill Capt.
Comdg 87th M.G. Coy.

APPENDIX I

N.C.O's & Men of the 84th Bde Machine Gun Coy, transferred to the M.G. Corps:-

N°	RANK	NAME	REMARKS
21276	C.S.M.	WHITE, F.J.	
21277	Sgt.	WINCH, H.	
21278	Cpl.	CHANT, E.	
21279	L. Cpl	JONES, H.	
21280	L. Cpl	COOKE, F.	
21281	L. Cpl	KING, R.	
21282	L. Cpl	COLLINS, H.	
21283	Pte.	PEARSON, J.	
21284	"	JESSON, H.	
21285	"	JONES, A.	
21286	"	MUSKER, C.	
21287	"	GARDINER, W.	
21288	"	DAVIES, A.	
21289	"	JONES, C.	
21290	"	BROAD, D.	
21291	"	PLEECE, E.	
21292	"	PORTSMOUTH, G.	From 2nd S.W.B's, 1/2/16. Authority G.O.C. 84th Inf. Bde. N° 670, 20/4/16
21293	"	BELCHER, S.	
21294	"	VICKERY, W.	
21295	"	STRANGE, W.	
21296	"	TAYLOR, A.	
21297	"	HILL, J.	
21298	"	LUCAS, A.	
21299	"	DAVIS, A.	
21300	"	DAVIS, C.	
21301	"	HEYWOOD, T.	
21302	"	PHILLIPS, S.	
21303	"	DEAN, J.	
21304	"	HENDY, J.	
21305	"	GRAY, A.	
21306	"	PRICE, D.	
21307	"	PARRY, A.	
21308	"	VOUSDEN, S.	
21309	"	PREECE, A.	
21310	"	EDWARDS,	Date of transfer 31/3/16

Sheet 2

No.	Rank.	Name.	Remarks.
21311.	C.Q.M.S.	YOUNG, A	
21312.	Sgt.	PAXTON, L.	
21313.	Cpl.	NICHOLL, W.	
21314.	L.Cpl	MORRISON, T.	
21315.	"	KERR, J.	
21316.	"	McFARLANE, J.	
21317.	Pte.	BROUGH, G.	
21318.	"	DEWAR, J.C.	
21319.	"	SHANKLAND, W.	
21320.	"	HUTTON, R.	
21321.	"	SHARP, J.	
21322.	"	KEMP, W.	
21323.	"	DUNKLEY, F.	
21324.	"	JOBE, J.	
21325	"	DOWNIE, D.	
21326.	"	MILNE, K.	
21327	"	TONNER, H.	
21328.	"	ADAMSON, J.	
21329.	"	RICHARDSON, F.	From 1st K.O.S.B's 1/2/16.
21330.	"	HAYWARD, W.	Authority G.O.C. 87th Inf. Bde.,
21331.	"	NICHOLLS, J.	No. 670, dated 20/4/16
21332.	"	McLEAN, H.	
21333.	"	RUTHERFORD, G.	
21334.	"	MIDDLETON, H.	
21335.	"	GREGORY, J.	
21336.	"	CRAIG, H.	
21337	"	TUCKER, F.	
21338.	"	ARTHUR, R.	
21339.	"	HUMPHRIES, J.	
21340.	"	HUNTER, R.	
21341.		JENNER, A.	
21342.		MORRISON, J.	
21343.		CURRAN, E.	
21344.		HOBSON, J.	
21345.		CARRUTHERS, J.	
21346.		KERR, W.	
21347.	Cpl	FERGUSON.	Date of transfer 10/4/16
21348.	Pte.	LINTON,	" " " "
21349	"	KING,	" " " "
21350.	"	PUGH,	" " " "
21351	"	McNULTY,	" " " "
21352	"	SCOTT.	19/4/16.

Sheet 3

No	RANK	NAME	
21353	Sgt.	BUTCHER, L.	
21354	"	LOWTHER, H.	
21355	Cpl	LINTON, W.	
21356	L.Cpl	FOWLES, B.	
21357	"	TURNER, D.	
21358	"	BENNISON, T.	
21359	"	FINLAY, S.	
21360	"	SLEE, W.	
21361	Pte.	CULVER, F.	
21362	"	EDWARDS, W.	
21363	"	HYATT, T.	
21364	"	STUART, J.	
21365	"	SPENCER, A.	
21366	"	GOLDEN, G.	
21367	"	IRWIN, W.	
21368	"	PATTERSON, J.	
21369	"	THWAITES, M.	From 1st Border Regt., 1/2/16.
21370	"	TETSILL, C.	Authority G.O.C., 87th Inf. Bde.,
21371	"	EMERSON, T.	No. 670 dated 20/4/16.
21372	"	FOSTER, L.	
21373	"	GIBSON, T.	
21374	"	HARRIS, G.	
21375	"	ANDERSON, D.	
21376	"	BRUMWELL, J.	
21377	"	LEMMING, J.	
21378	"	BATEMAN, J.	
21379	"	SWIFT, F.	
21380	"	RODGERS, J.	
21381	"	HARPER, G.	
21382	"	WELSH, F.	
21383	"	WORSLEY, H.	
21384	"	HARKISS, W.	
21385	"	HARPER, G.	
21386	"	CATLEY, C.T.	

Sheet 4.

No.	RANK.	NAME.	
21384.	Sgt.	McATEER.	
21388.	"	DUFFIE, W.J.	
21389.	"	COLLINS, T.M.	
21390.	Cpl.	CREIGHTON, J.	
21391.	"	MELLEY, P.	
21392.	L.Cpl	MILLAR, J.	
21393.	"	McCANDLESS, J	
21394.	"	FAY, J.	
21396.	"	WALSH, T	
21399.	Pte	CUNNINGHAM, P.	
21400.	"	McNEICE, J.	
21401.	"	RIDLEY, W	
21402.	"	KYLE, W	From 1st Royal Inniskilling Fus., 1/2/16.
21403.	"	SLATER, G.	Authority G.O.C., 84th Inf. Bde.,
21406.	"	STAVERS, S.	No. 670 dated 20/4/16.
21407.	"	MEEHAN, C.	
21408.	"	FARNIN, J.	
21411.	"	SLOAN, T.	
21412.	"	STOREY, W	
21413	"	BURNAGE, E.	
21414.	"	FORBES, T	
21415	"	ROBB, P.	
21416.	"	AMBROSE, H.	
21417	"	DRUMGOON,	
21418.	L.Cpl	COLLINS, J	
21419	Pte	RADCLIFFE, W.	

Appendix 2.   Nº 13 Copy.

SECRET.   No 1

Operation Order by Capt. H.R. Burrell Commdg.
87th Bde. Machine Gun Coy.

All references to MAP 1/20000 57 D.S.E. and 1/10000 Trench Map
Sheet 57 D.S.E. BEAUMONT 1 & 2. (Parts of).

----

(1). A general attack will take place on the German positions on a date which will be notified later, & which will be indicated in future instructions by the letter Z.

It will be preceded for several days by a steady bombardment. Gas will be discharged at intervals during the bombardment, if the wind is favourable.

(2). During the bombardment, Lewis Gun, Machine Gun and Rifle fire will be kept up by night to prevent the enemy repairing the damage done to their wire.

(3). The 1st R. Inniskilling Fusrs. and the 2nd S.W. Borderers will assault the first line system of trenches. These battalions will move out of their trenches in sufficient time to bring them 100 yds. short of the enemy's trenches in the required formation and alignment at the hour detailed for the assault.

The boundaries allotted to the Brigade are:—

Southern: Point 03. (Q.17.b.15.4) inclusive — Q.17.b.2.35. —
Point 83 (Q.17.b.8.3.) — Station Buildings (Q.18.b.7.6) last three exclusive.

Northern. Point 89. (Q.10.d.55.70.) Exclusive. Y Ravine inclusive.

(4). Second Objective. The 1st K.O.S.B.s and 1st Border Regt. will assault the BEAUCOURT RIDGE position. They will leave their trenches as soon as the last wave of the leading battalions has reached the enemy's wire, & move down to the Station Road, forming up for the further advance between railway and Station Alleys.

The objective of the Brigade is from Point R.7.c.9.4. to the N. end of BEAUCOURT REDOUBT (Point 7549) both inclusive.

(5). Signal for Assault. The Signal for the assault will be a series of blasts on the Whistle given by the O.C. Company and repeated by all Platoon & Section Commanders.

(6) Reserve Brigade. As soon as the Brigade has captured the BEAUCOURT RIDGE, the 88th Brigade will pass through and assault the PUISIEUX TRENCH.

(7). When the 88th Brigade has passed through, the 1st R. Innis. Fus. will reorg-ise in the vicinity of the STATION ROAD, E of Station Alley, &

become the Brigade Reserve.

The 2nd S.W.B.'s will take over the consolidation of the whole first line system.

(8). <u>Units on Flanks</u>. Simultaneously with the advance of the 87th Brigade the 36th Division will advance on our right and the 86th Brigade on our left.

(9). During the attack <u>Machine Guns</u> able to use direct fire will support the attack on BEAUCOURT REDOUBT by overhead fire. No overhead fire will be used after our troops have reached BEAUCOURT REDOUBT.

(10). <u>Underground Galleries</u>. The underground galleries running forward from MARY REDAN and 1st Avenue will be broken through by the Tunnelling Coy: on the Z morning. These will only be used by Officers, Runners, and for laying telephone wires and water pipes.

(11). <u>Reserve Troops</u>. After the advance, a Brigade Reserve will move forward & occupy our front line trenches with a view to guarding against a counter-attack, rallying stragglers and taking over prisoners. They will hold that portion of the line usually held by their battalions and will send an officer from each battalion to Brigade H.Q's to report their arrival. They will be prepared to carry forward ammunition, water & stores, to their respective battalions as required.

(12) <u>Aircraft</u>. Two aeroplanes will be employed continuously as Contact Patrols. Communication with them will be carried out in accordance with instructions previously issued under C.G.S. 44. dated 1st June, 1916.

(13) Every Infantry Soldier will wear a triangular piece of tin, 4" sides, between the shoulders. Each platoon will be issued with a Diamond-shaped screen red & yellow halves. These will be erected to mark the most forward position reached by the platoon.

(14) <u>Trench Traffic</u>. On & after Z morning WITHINGTON, TIPPERARY, and 2nd AVENUE will be used for UP traffic only. GABION, BROADWAY and 3rd AVENUE for DOWN traffic only. N.B. UP = <u>to</u> trenches; DOWN = <u>FROM</u> trenches. Staff Officers & telephone linesmen only may use them both ways.

(15). <u>Equipment & Stores</u>. In addition to Secret List issued previously each man will carry S.A.A. 120 rounds; Rations for day of attack & 1 Iron Ration; Steel Helmet; 1 GAS Helmet (latest pattern) in Satchel; 1 Box Respirator; Water Bottle & Haversack.

(16). <u>KITS</u> - Officers' Equipment, men's kit, & Dixies will be stored at Q.M. Stores in ENGLEBELMER, & will be handed in prior to moving up to trenches. A sandbag will be drawn from Q.M. Stores for each man, for surplus kit & will be labelled clearly with the owner's number & name.

(17). All bayonets will be sharpened.

(18). MEDICAL. Advanced Dressing Stations will be established at KNIGHTSBRIDGE and VITERMONT CHURCH. Fighting troops are forbidden to accompany wounded to the dressing stations.

(19). Prisoners. All prisoners will be handed over to the 2nd S.W.B's who will in turn hand them over to the 10% reserve remaining in our front line trenches.

(20). DUMPS. MAP showing position of all forward Dumps may be seen at the Orderly Room.

(21). MAPS. The only Maps that will be carried in the attack or referred to in messages will be the 1/10000 BEAUMONT, Trench Map Sheet 57 D.S., and 1/20000 Sheet 57 D.S.E. shewing the German trenches & not our own. No other Maps or papers will be carried. All Officers & N.C.O's will carry note books.

(22). WATCHES. Watches will be synchronised at 9.30 A.M. and 7.30 P.M. on X & Y days. All officers will send their watches to Coy. H.Q. at these hours to be set.

(23). The Brigade Hdqrs. will be in FETHARD STREET between HARROW ROAD and PRAED STREET. The C.O. will be here throughout the operations.

G.H. Moberly
2Lt. & adjt.
87th M.G. Coy.

June 19th 1916.
   Issued at
     Copy No 1, 2 = Office
            3 = Lt Cayley
            4 = " Costello
            5 = 2/Lt Breene
            6 = " Hunter.
            7 = " Marsh.
            8 = " Green.
            9 = " Cranfield
           10 = " Farrant.
           11 = " Outwin.
           12 = " Ledward.
           13 = War Diary.

SECRET

Headquarters
87th Bde. M.G. Coy.

Each Gun Team consists of an N.C.O. and 5 men. With an additional detachment of 7 men per Gun, the Gun & ammunition would be carried as follows:—

N.C.O.	2 Belt boxes
1.	Gun & light tripod, oil can
2.	2 Belt boxes, condenser, oil can.
3.	Spare parts box & pick.
4.	2 Belt boxes.
5.	Tin of water (2 galls) & Shovel.
6.	2 Belt boxes & Rangefinder.
7, 8, 9.	2 Belt boxes.
10.	Heavy Tripod.
11 & 12.	700 rounds each, carried loose in pack.

Each man carries 3 sandbags. Extra water bottles taken if available.

N.R. Burell   Capt.
Commdg. 87th Bde. M.G. Coy.

APPENDIX 3.

Index to Copies of OPERATION ORDER No 2.

Copy No 1, 2 to Office
" " 3 " War Diary.
" " 4 " Lt CAYLEY. D.C.
" " 5 " " COSTELLO. E.W.
" " 6 " 2nd Lt BREENE. T.F.
" " 7 " " " MARSH. R.N.C.
" " 8 " " " ~~[struck through]~~ OUTWIN. S.G.
" " 9 " " " LEDWARD. H.P
" " 10 " " " CRANFIELD. R.E
" " 11 " " " HUNTER. J.H.D
" " 12 " " " FARRANT. A.W
" " 13 " " " GREEN. R.C
" " 14 " C.S.M WHITE. F.J.

June 21st 1916.

E. Mosberly. 2nd Lt & Adjt

87th Bde Machine Gun Coy.

SECRET

Copy No 3

OPERATION ORDER No 2

by Capt. J.R. Burrill, Commdg. 87th Bde. Machine Gun Coy.

(1). <u>Boundary on Right Flank</u>:— The dividing line between the 87th Inf. Brigade and 36th Division will be as follows instead of as detailed in previous orders. "A line from the point of MARY REDAN (Q.17.a.50.30) to houses at R.y.c.20.05., thence to Railway and along railway to R.8.d.30.85. The houses and the Railway Line are inclusive to 36th Division.

(2). <u>Bombardment</u>. The bombardment will last for 5 days which are denoted by the letters U. V. W. X. and Y.

(3). <u>GAS</u>. A discharge of gas will take place on V/W night should the wind be favourable, or on the first subsequent night, when the weather conditions are favourable. Detailed instructions are attached. Vide APPENDIX "A".

(4) <u>SMOKE</u>. A discharge of smoke along our front will take place at intervals during the preliminary bombardment, but it will not be commenced until after the gas has been discharged, consequently "W" is the first day on which smoke will be used. Detailed instructions are attached. Vide APPENDIX "B".

(5). <u>Reconnoitring Wire</u>.

(a) There will be no Artillery Fire on the front between the hours named below:—

V/W.	11 p.m. to 12 midnight.
W/X.	10.30 p.m. to 11.30 p.m.
X/Y.	12 midnight to 1. a.m.
Y/Z.	11.30. p.m. to 12.30 p.m.

Rifle, Lewis & Machine Gun Fire on the enemy's front will cease during the above named hours. Battalions holding the front line will send out patrols at these hours to examine the wire and will send in reports by 7 a.m. the following morning as to the state of the wire. During the remainder of these nights the enemy's wire will be kept under fire.

(b). The Officers detailed to reconnoitre the enemy's wire will be present all day at the OBSERVATION POSTS of the Wire-cutting Batteries.

(c). The Artillery Group Commanders will notify Battalion Commanders of the date and time appointed for the wire-cutting, together with the positions of the Observation Posts to be used

(d) Machine Gun Officers will report to Battalion Commanders, & will enquire at what hours & what areas the Artillery are wire-cutting. These areas need not be covered by M.G. Fire during that time.

(6) <u>Deep Dug-outs</u>.

All men not on duty with the Guns must be kept in deep dug-outs whenever possible. Guns will only be put in position at dusk and removed at dawn.

Army Book 417.

Certificate to be Signed before Fire is Opened.

1. I have checked all calculations and line of fire of gun.
2. The Brigadier-General commanding the line of trenches, i.e., Nos. _____, has sanctioned fire from _____ date.
3. The troops occupying trenches No. _____ have been notified.

(Signed) _____ B.M.G.O.

Officer in charge of Gun _____ Sheet _____ Square _____

(7). <u>Programme of Attack</u>:- A detailed programme of the Infantry Advance & Artillery Lifts is attached. Vide APPENDIX "C".

(8). <u>STOKES MORTARS</u> - The Stokes Trench Mortars in the Tunnel Emplacements will open a Hurricane Bombardment at a rate not exceeding 25 rounds per minute, on the targets already notified at precisely 10 minutes before the hour fixed for the assault (i.e. -10.)
The Mortars will cease fire at the hour fixed of the assault (i.e. 00), except those mortars specially furnished with red cartridges, which will continue to fire for another two minutes (i.e. from 00 - 02), using these cartridges at the enemy's support trenches.

(9). <u>S.O.S. Signal</u>. The S.O.S. Signal either by day or night will be 5 Red Rockets in quick succession. Battalions will carry 15 of these Rockets in case the forward objectives are not attained.

(10). <u>Bombers' Flags</u>. One man in each bombing squad will carry a Flag one foot square, with a vertical division, Red one half & Yellow the other half, on a 6' stick. These flags will be carried and must never be planted in the ground. They must be held up over the parapet to indicate the most forward position reached by the squad. 16 flags will be issued to each Battalion.

APPENDIX "A".
Arrangements for GAS DISCHARGE.

(1) 400 Cylinders of White Star Gas will be installed prior to the bombardment in 20 emplacements on the 29th Division Front between Q.10/2 and Q.10/12. Each emplacement will hold 20 cylinders.

(2). The <u>programme of discharge</u> will be as under on V/W night or subsequent nights:-
 (a). Hour fixed - 0.4 ------- 4 cylinders simultaneously per Bay.
 (b). From 0.4 - 1.24 ------- 8 cylinders per Bay discharged one at a time every 10 minutes
 (c). At 1.24 ------------ 8 cylinders per Bay simultaneously.

(3). The "hour fixed" will be notified shortly after 5p.m. on the evening before the discharge, & no discharge will take place without the direct authority of the Corps.

(4). Machine Gun Officers will report to Battalion H.Qrs. at 5p.m. & obtain the hour fixed for discharge. Box Respirators will be put on by all 5 minutes before the hour fixed for discharge, & will only be removed on the authority of the M.G.O. who will satisfy himself that no gas remains in the vicinity. Vermorel Sprayers should be used, if necessary, to clear Dug-outs & emplacements of Gas.

(5). Just before & during the discharge at "hour fixed" and 1.24. Battalions holding the front line will arrange for rifle & machine gun fire to be maintained to drown the noise of the discharging gas.

(6). Men not on duty will be placed in deep Dug-outs.

(2661.) Wt. 12834.—M 30. 200 M. 12/15. J. T. & S., Ltd. Army Book 417.

Certificate to be Signed before Fire is Opened.

1. I have checked all calculations and line of fire of gun.
2. The Brigadier-General commanding the line of trenches, i.e., Nos. .... has sanctioned fire from .... to .... date.
3. The troops occupying trenches No. .... have been notified.

.... (Signed) .... B.M.G.O.

Officer in charge of Gun ....   Sheet .... Square ....

(v) The following code will be used in connection with the Gas Discharge:-
   (i). Wind is favourable for discharge of Gas — — — — — — — "Berlin"
   (ii). Wind is not favourable for discharge of Gas — — — — — — "Hanover"
   (iii). Is wind favourable for discharge of Gas — — — — — — "Cologne"
   (iv). Discharge Gas at — — — — — — — — — — — — — "Dresden"

APPENDIX "B"
Arrangements for Smoke Discharge.

1. Stations for the discharge of Smoke will be placed at intervals of about 25 yards along the Brigade Front. There will be about 40 Stations in all.
   Two men will be allotted to each station.
   The special Brigade R.E. are supplying 30 men to assist, & Battalions holding the line will make up the balance to the Total required.

2. The men selected by Battalions for throwing the Smoke Bombs need not be specially skilled, as all instruction that is needful will be given by the Special Brigade.

3. The following numbers of candles will be discharged on each day should the weather permit:-

   "W" day   2400 candles   400
   "X" day (morning)   2400   "   400
   "X" day (evening)   2400   "   400
   "Y" day (morning)   2400   "   400
   "Y" day (evening)   2400   "   400

4. The discharge will last for 10 minutes and will take place at the following times:-
   "W" day   from 10.15 a.m. — 10.25 a.m.
   "X" day (morning) from 5.45 a.m. — 5.55 a.m. and again
   "X" day (evening) from 6.55 p.m. — 7.5 p.m.
   "Y" day (morning) from 7.15 a.m. — 7.25 a.m. and again
   "Y" day (evening) from 5.15 p.m. — 5.25 p.m.

   These times have been arranged to coincide with the special Artillery bombardment which will take place on those days.

5. All men except one per gun team on observation, will be placed in deep dug-outs, to avoid the enemy's barrage which the smoke will probably draw.

6. The discharge will be carried out under the direction of the officer of the special Brigade R.E. — 2nd Lieut. Pheasey. R.E.

Army Book 417.

Certificate to be Signed before Fire is Opened.

1. I have checked all calculations and line of fire of gun.
2. The Brigadier-General commanding the line of trenches, i.e., Nos. _____ has sanctioned fire from _____ to _____ date.
3. The troops occupying trenches No. _____ have been notified.

(Signed) _____ B. M. G. O.

Officer in charge of Gun _____ Sheet _____ Square _____

7. The decision as to whether smoke is to be discharged will be sent from Divisional Headquarters, & in the event of the wind changing or becoming unfavourable the Officer mentioned in (6) is authorised to countermand the discharge.

APPENDIX "C".

Programme of Infantry Advance & Artillery Bombardment.

Time	Moves of Infantry.	Trench Mortars.	Divl. Artillery.	Heavy Artillery
-10.		Stokes' Mortars open hurricane bombardment.		
-5.				Lift on to line Q.12.d.45.1. — Q.12.c.7.1. — Q.12.c.1.4. — Q.11.b.1.5. — Q.5.c.85.05. — Q.5.d.4.4. —
0.0.	87th & 86th Bdes. assault 1st objective & advance at rate not exceeding 50 yards a minute.	All Trench Mortars cease fire. Stokes' Mortars, if Red Cartridges received, lift to support lines.	Lift to enemy support trench, or minimum of 100 yds. beyond front line.	
0.2.		Stokes Mortars cease fire.	Lift another 100 yds.	
0.4.			Lift another 100 yds. & continue lifting at rate of 100 yds. every 2 minutes until they reach the Station & Wagon Roads.	
0.15.				Lift on to 2nd objective.
0.20.	87th & 86th Bdes. reach Station & Wagon Roads.		Lift 150 yds. East of Station & Wagon Roads, & remain there till 1.00.	
1.00.	87th & 86th Bdes. advance from Station & Wagon Rds. against 2nd objective at rate not exceeding 50 yds. a minute.		Lift 100 yards.	

Army Book 417.

Certificate to be Signed before Fire is Opened.

1. I have checked all calculations and line of fire of gun.
2. The Brigadier-General commanding the line of trenches, i.e., Nos. _____, has sanctioned fire from _____ to _____ date.
3. The troops occupying trenches No. _____ have been notified.

(Signed) _____ B.M.G.O.

Officer in charge of Gun _____ Sheet _____ Square _____

Time.	Moves of Infantry.	Trench Mortars.	Divl. Artillery.	Heavy Artillery.
1.2.			Lift another 100 yds & continue lifting at this rate until they reach Beaucourt Ridge Trenches, where they remain till 1.20.	
1.15.				Lift on to Beaucourt Village.
1.20.	87th & 86th Bdes assault 2nd Objective.		Lift on to line of wire R.7.a.5.2. to R.1.c.25.50. (where they remain until 1.35) & also on to Beaucourt village.	
1.25.				Lift to 3rd objective.
1.30.	87th & 86th Bdes. send out patrols to cut line of wire R.7.a.5.2. to R.1.c.25.50. 87th Bde assault Beaucourt Village.		Lift off Beaucourt Village.	
1.35.	87th & 86th Bdes cut wire.		Lift off line of wire to East of Artillery Lane & maintain barrage until 2.30.	
2.30.	88th Bde. advance through wire to PUISIEUX ROAD at rate not exceeding 50 yds per minute.		Lift to the PUISIEUX ROAD.	
2.40.	88th Bde. reach PUISIEUX ROAD.		Lift 100 yds & continue lifting at rate of 100 yds every 2 minutes, until they reach line of wire R.2.d.1.15 to R.2.a.6.0. and BOIS D'HOLLANDE (R.8.a.) where they remain till 3.00.	
3.00.			Lift on 3rd Objective & remain there until 3.30.	
3.10.	88th Bde. advance from Puisieux Rd towards 3rd objective.			
3.25.	88th Bde assault 3rd Objective		Lift 300 yds beyond enemys support line & barrage until 4.30	Lift on to BAILLESCOURT and gun positions.
3.30.				
4.30.			Barrage ceases.	

J.H. Moberly
2Lt tg adjt
87th M.G. Coy
21/6/16.

(2681.) Wt. 18684.—M 30. 200 M. 12/15. J, T. & S., Ltd.   Army Book 417.

Certificate to be Signed before Fire is Opened.

1. I have checked all calculations and line of fire of gun.
2. The Brigadier-General commanding the line of trenches, i.e., Nos. _____, has sanctioned fire from _____ to _____ date.
3. The troops occupying trenches No. _____ have been notified.

(Signed) _____   _____ B.M.G.O.

Officer in charge of Gun _____   Sheet _____ Square _____

SECRET

Appendix 4.

Copy No. 3.

OPERATION ORDER No. 3.

by Capt. H.R. Burrill, Comdg. 87th Bde. Machine Gun Coy.

Allocation of Guns. — No. 1. SECTION.

A. No. 1 & 2 Gun Teams under 2nd Lt. T.F. BREENE attached to 2/S.W.B's. will go forward with reserve Coy. & occupy positions in 1st Objective to sweep Beaucourt Redoubt & so assist the advance of the 1st Border Regt. with overhead fire. Guns will cease overhead fire as soon as assaulting troops reach limit of safety. 2 degrees of safety will be used. [Tangent sight raised 400 yds]. These guns should be prepared to cover the left flank in case of counter-attack from Beaumont Hamel.

B. No. 3 & 4 Gun Teams under 2/Lt HUNTER will occupy FETHARD ST. LEFT & THURLES' DUMP prior to the Bombardment. FETHARD ST. LEFT will fire each night at German 1st & 2nd lines from Q.10.B.72 to Q.17.a.97. and German 3rd line from (85) Q.11.c.85. to (00) Q.11.d.00. THURLES' DUMP will fire each night at German 1st, 2nd, & 3rd lines from Q.17.b.42. to Railway. [During 1/2 night THURLES' DUMP Gun will be moved & occupy a position in FETHARD ST.. 2/LT HUNTER will report when this has been done.

- 0.30. Before attack sweep German Front Lines
- 0.10. Left Gun on Beaumont Alley — Right on Station Alley.
- 0.20. Lift on to BEAUCOURT REDOUBT.
- 1.05. Cease fire.

No. 2 SECTION.

A. No. 1 & 2 Gun Teams under Lt. CAYLEY attached to 1st K.O.S.B. will go forward with Reserve Coy. & occupy positions in BEAUCOURT to consolidate the village, & assist the advance of the 88th Infantry Bde. on PUISIEUX TRENCH. These guns should be prepared to cover right flank from Counter-attack & to support 1st Border Regt. on Left.

B. No. 3 & 4 Gun Teams under 2/Lieut. R.N.C. MARSH will occupy SHOOTERS' HILL Q.17.c.30.15. & Q.17.c.6.1. prior to the Bombardment. These guns will fire each night on German 1st & 2nd line from Q.17.b.0.5 to Q.17.b.9.1.

- 0.30. Sweep German Front Lines.
- 0.10. Left Gun — RAILWAY ALLEY; RIGHT GUN — STATION ALLEY.
- 0.20. Fire on BEAUCOURT VILLAGE
- 1.05. Cease fire.

No. 3. SECTION.

A. No. 1 & 2 Gun Teams under Lt. COSTELLO attached 1st Royal Innis. Fus. will go forward with Reserve Coy. & occupy positions in 1st objective to sweep BEAUCOURT village & to assist advance of 1/K.O.S.B. with overhead fire. Guns will cease overhead fire as soon as assaulting troops reach limit of safety. 2 degrees of safety (Tangent sight raised 400 yds) will be used

These guns will be prepared to cover the Right Flank of both 1st & 2nd Objectives in case of Counter-attack.

When the 1/Royal Innis. Fus. re-organise & become Brigade Reserve, these two Guns will remain in position & be attached to 2/S.W.B.s.

B. No 3 & 4 Gun Teams under 2/Lt R.C.GREEN will occupy positions at Sap 3 and Sap 2 prior to the Bombardment. These Guns will fire each night at German 1st & 2nd lines from Q.10.b.7.2. to Q.17.a.8.8. and German 3rd line from Q.11.c.4.9. to Q.11.c.9.3.

- 0·30. Sweep German Front Lines.
- 0·10. Sap 3 — BEAUMONT ALLEY ; Sap 2 — STATION ALLEY.
  0·20 — BEAUCOURT VILLAGE (both Guns).
  1·05   Cease Fire.

No 4. SECTION.

A. No 2 & 3 Gun Teams under 2/Lt CRANFIELD, attached 1/Border Regt. will go forward with the Reserve Coy. & occupy positions in 2nd Objective, and sweep ARTILLERY ALLEY and PUISIEUX TRENCH, & so assist the advance of the 88th Bde. with Overhead Fire.

Guns will cease Overhead Fire as soon as assaulting troops have reached limit of safety. 2 degrees of safety (Tangent sight raised 400 yds) will be used.

These Guns should be prepared to cover Left flank in case of Counter-attack, & if necessary to support 1/K.O.S.B.s on Right.

B. Nos 1 & 4 Gun Teams under 2/Lt FARRANT will occupy F.5e & D.5e prior to the Bombardment. These Guns will fire on German 1st Line from pt (89) Q.10.d.6.8 to Q.17.a.8.7, & on German 2nd & 3rd lines from pt (85) Q.11.c.8.5. to pt (00) Q.11.d.0.0.

- 0·30 Sweep German Front Line.
- 0·10 BEAUMONT ALLEY.
  0·20 BEAUCOURT REDOUBT.
  1·05 Cease Fire.

II. RATE OF FIRE:- During hours Guns are firing, every Gun will fire at least 1 Belt every 20 minutes.

III. WIRE PATROLS. No Gun need fire at trenches when Artillery are cutting wire in front of those trenches.

No Guns will fire during the hours laid down for reconnoitring wire in Coy. OPERATION ORDER No 2. para 5a.

IV. OVERHEAD FIRE. Guns using Overhead Fire will not fire at any trenches or ground within 250 yds. of Station Road.

V. PRECAUTIONS. After the whistles have sounded for the troops to leave our trenches prior to the assault, an officer or Sgt. must be with each Gun in action to ensure that the Gun ceases fire whenever troops leaving our trenches are likely to pass in front of the Gun within the Dangerous Zone.

VI. Carrying Parties. All Machine Gun Teams will have 7 men per Gun Team attached for carrying purposes. Those Gun Teams attached to Batt'ns will be supplied by those Batt'ns & the remaining 8 Gun Teams will have 7 men attached from the Brigade Reserve mentioned in Coy. Operation Order No. 1. para. 11., on the arrival of Bde. Reserve in the Front Line trenches. The 8 Gun Teams must be prepared to advance immediately the 7 men per Gun Team arrive. 1 man per Half Section will report to C.O. at Bde. H'd Q'rs at 2:00 to act as guide.

VII. DEEP DUG-OUTS. All men not required to fire the Gun or carry ammunition must be kept under cover & if possible in deep dug-outs.

VIII. AMMUNITION. Officers i/c Machine Guns are responsible for knowing the position of all AMM. DUMPS, & replacing AMM. expended. Officers i/c M. Guns attached to Batt'ns, immediately on reaching the objective, will send the carrying parties to collect AMM. if possible from Batt'n H'd Q'rs., or otherwise from AMM. DUMPS in our own Front Line.

IX. WATER :- A plentiful supply of water must be maintained at each Gun. Till Z-day this will be obtained from Water Dumps, and afterwards will normally be obtained from the RIVER ANCRE.

X. RATIONS :- Gun Teams attached to Batt'ns will continue to draw rations from those Batt'ns until noon on (Z + 2) day [i.e. 2 days after Z day]. The remaining Gun Teams under O.C. Machine Gun Coy. will draw rations from junction of GABION AVENUE and KNIGHTSBRIDGE BARRACKS. Only one man per 2 Gun Teams will normally be sent.
Carrying parties attached to Gun Teams will be rationed throughout by their respective Batt'ns.

XI.(a) A small Coy. Dump will be formed in the Deep Dug-out of SAP 2. Gun. It will include the following :- Metal Belts (large & small), Field Dressings, Flannelette, Oil Lubricating, Gas Helmets with Satchels, Goggles weeping, Candles, various spare parts.
(b). Officers commanding Half Sections will report to H'd Q'rs as soon as possible where all their spare kit, etc., has been dumped.

XII. COMMUNICATION. Telephones will be laid to SHOOTERS' HILL, SAP 2, THURLES' DUMP, & F. S'n. A Signaller will be detailed for duty at each station. When the THURLES' DUMP Gun is moved to FETHARD S't on Y/Z night, the Signaller on duty at THURLES' DUMP will report with instrument to C.O. at Bde. H'd Q'rs.

XIII **DUMP.** The Dump for the Coy. has been fixed in the grounds of PETIT CHATEAU in ACHEUX. P.13.6.8.4. (DIV: SCHOOL of INSTRUCTION).
All stores will be dumped under the following headings –

(i). To Go Forward.   (ii) To be Sent Back.

(3). For Baggage Wagons. – Officers' Kits, Men's Kits, Dixies.

Stores for Dumps (i) & (ii) will be collected in following categories.

(a). Ordnance Stores.   (b). A.S.C. Stores.   (c). R.E. Stores.

(d) Medical Stores   (e). Veterinary Stores.

Stores for Dump (3) must be labelled distinctly. Lists showing what is dumped under each heading will be sent to TOWN COMMANDANT, ACHEUX & LT ANDERSON i/c 87th Bde. Salvage Co.

No. 21301 Pte. HEYWOOD, Coy. Sanitary Man, will be in charge of the Coy. Stores at the above Dump.

———✕———

Copy Nos 1 & 2 – Office.
          3 – War Diary.
          4 – 87th Bde.
          5 – 2nd S.W.B.
          6 – 1st K.O.S.B.
          7 – 1st R.I.F.
          8 – 1st Border.
          9 – 86th Bde. M.G. Coy.
        10 – 88th Bde. M.G. Coy.
        11 – 2nd LT Breene. T.F.
        12 – " " Hunter. J.H.D.
        13 – LT Cayley. D.C.
        14 – 2nd LT Marsh. R.N.C.
        15 – LT Costello. E.W.
        16 – 2nd LT Green. R.C.
        17 – " " Cranfield. R.E.
        18 – " " Farrant. A.W.
        19 – " " Ledward. H.P.
        20 – " " Outram. S.G.
        21 – C.S.M. White. F.J.

G.H. Moberly
2Lt & a/Capt
87th Bde Machine Gun Coy.

June 23rd 1916
    Issued at 13:00

Appendix 5.

Scale: 1 in 10,000.

Reference: BEAUMONT Trench Map.
57D S.E. 1 & 2 (parts of)

Nº 1 gun = "F Street"
— 2 — = "D Street"
— 3 — = "THURLES DUMP" (afterwards moved to CARLISLE ST)
— 4 — = "FETHARD ST"
— 5 — = "OLD FIRING LINE"
— 6 — = "SAP 2"
— 7 & 8 = "SHOOTER'S HILL"

1/1 = Gun Positions.

SECRET   87th Bde. Machine Gun Coy.   Operation Order No 4.

APPENDIX 6   June 25th 1916

Reference:- Trench Map 1/10000 BEAUMONT.
                    57 D. S E 1 & 2 (parts of)

I. It is intended to carry out a raid on the German trenches on the night W/X.

II. Point of Entry.- Between point 7347 (Q.10.D.7,45) and Q.11.C.1.35.

III. Point of Exit. 4 bays right of Sap 3 to 4 bays left of Sap 3.

IV. Time Table. 23.30 Raiding party leaves our trenches and forms up in "NO MAN'S LAND" 150x from enemy's wire.

    01,00 Raiding party leave the German trenches and go back to our own trenches if they can. If they cannot do this owing to enemy's fire, they will lie up in "NO MAN'S LAND" at their original forming up place, until such time as they can return to our trenches.

    01,15 M.G's cease fire.

V. Machine Guns. 2 Machine Guns under 2/Lt FARRANT will place a barrage across "NO MAN'S LAND" between our trenches and point 89, and 2 Machine Guns under 2/Lt GREEN will place a similar barrage between our trenches and point 54, in order to prevent any Germans leaving their trenches and taking the raiding party in flank.

    The M. Guns under 2/Lt HUNTER will not fire during the raid, except THURLE'S DUMP Gun, which will fire at German trenches in Q 17 b and Q 17 a. (as usual)

    The 2 M. Guns under 2/Lt MARSH will fire as usual.

    2/Lt FARRANT and 2/Lt GREEN will see that their guns are placed well to the flanks of the points of exit of the raiding party.

                                    G. H. Moberly
                                    2Lt. + Adjt.
                                    87th Bde Machine Gun Coy

SECRET.   APPENDIX 47.   Copy No. 2

87th Bde Machine Gun Company
Operation Order No. 5.

In the Field
29th June 1916

1.) Zero having been postponed 48 hours, to-day 29th June will be called "Y1" day.
   30th June will be called "Y2" day
   1st July will be Z day.

2.) No alterations in the present disposition of the B.G. will be made.

3.) Concentrated bombardments by the Artillery will take place as follows:—
   "Y1" day ..... 4 p.m. — 5.20 p.m.
   "Y2" day ..... 8 A.M. — 9.20 A.M.

4.) There will be no Machine Gun Fire during the following hours for reconnoitring wire:—
   "Y1" day .... 10.30 p.m. — 11.30 p.m.
   "Y2" day .... 11 p.m. — 12 midnight.

5.) The programme for Z day will be as originally arranged.

6.) Please acknowledge.

J.H. Moberly
2Lt +adjt.
87th Bde Machine Gun Coy

Copy No. 1 = Office
  — 2 = War Diary
  — 3 = 2Lt Hunter
  — 4 = 2Lt Marsh
  — 5 = 2nd Lt Green
  — 6 = 2nd Lt Farrant.

29th Division.
87th Infantry Brigade.
- ----

87th MACHINE GUN COMPANY

JULY 1916

Appendices attached :- Operations Orders.
Special Orders of the Day

CONFIDENTIAL.

Vol 2

War Diary
of
87th M.G. Coy.

Volume II.

From July 1st 1916. To July 31st 1916.

Army Form C. 2118

WAR DIARY
or
INTELLIGENCE SUMMARY
(Erase heading not required.)

Instructions regarding War Diaries and Intelligence Summaries are contained in F.S. Regs., Part II. and the Staff Manual respectively. Title Pages will be prepared in manuscript.

Place	Date	Hour	Summary of Events and Information	Remarks and references to Appendices
ENGLEBELMER SECTOR	July 1st		87th M.G. Coy (less 8 guns attached to Btns) co-operated in attack on German lines at 7:30 A.M. Fire was maintained in accordance with Appendix 4 of June War Diary. At SHOOTER'S HILL 1 gun of No 2 Section opened fire about 8 A.m. on parties of Germans seen standing on parapet & firing on our own attacking troops. At FETHARD St LEFT, fire was opened at 7.35 A.M. on parties of enemy retreating near STATION ALLEY. For Casualties see Appendix 1. In the evening 88th M.G. Coy (less 8 guns) relieved 87th M.G. Coy, No 4 Section & No 2 Section & ½ No 3 Section occupying the REDOUBT LINE. The remainder were held in readiness near junction of UXBRIDGE ROAD & ST JOHN'S ROAD.	App. I.
	July 2nd		8 guns attached to Btns rejoined the Coy. 87th Bde. took over the sector from right of MARY REDAN to river ANCRE. 87th M.G. Coy took over gun positions in this sector from 106th M.G. Coy, Coy H.Qrs being in HAMEL.	
	July 3rd		Casualties: 2nd Lt R.N.C. MARSH Killed R.E. CRANFIELD wounded	

Army Form C. 2118

WAR DIARY
or
INTELLIGENCE SUMMARY

(Erase heading not required.)

Instructions regarding War Diaries and Intelligence Summaries are contained in F. S. Regs., Part II. and the Staff Manual respectively. Title Pages will be prepared in manuscript.

Place	Date	Hour	Summary of Events and Information	Remarks and references to Appendices
ENGLEBELMER SECTOR	July 4th		Casualties: 1 O.R. wounded. Message from Lt. Genl. Sir A. HUNTER WESTON (scies).	See App. 2.
"	July 8th		Coy relieved by 86th M.G. Coy, & went back to ENGLEBELMER to rest. 2nd Lt. D.T. JENKINS taken on strength of Coy. Coy divided into 8 sections instead of 4, to be known in future as 1A, 1B, 2A, 2B etc.	
ENGLEBELMER	July 9th		2nd Lt. T.C. BENNETT taken on strength of Coy.	
"	July 10th		No 21418 Cpl. COLLINS, No 21295 Pte LUCAS, No 18129 Pte EVANS recommended for D.C.M. for distinguished conduct on July 1st.	
"	July 12th		Special Reconnaissance of ENGLEBELMER. Scheme for defence of ENGLEBELMER sent in to 29th Division.	
"	July 14th		Draft of 1 Cpl and 14 men from GRANTHAM taken on strength of Coy. Fighting strength of Coy 11 officers, 136 other ranks.	
"	July 15th		Coy relieved 88th M.G. Coy in left sub sector, Coy HdQrs being at ENGLEBELMER. Special Order of the Day issued.	See App. 3.

WAR DIARY or INTELLIGENCE SUMMARY

Army Form C. 2118

(Erase heading not required.)

Instructions regarding War Diaries and Intelligence Summaries are contained in F.S. Regs., Part II. and the Staff Manual respectively. Title Pages will be prepared in manuscript.

Place	Date	Hour	Summary of Events and Information	Remarks and references to Appendices
ENGLEBELMER	July 20th		Reconnaissance made by order of 87th Bde. to decide on M.G. positions — 8 forward + 8 rear — to enfilade German front line. Report on this sent in to Bde.	
	July 21st		Further reconnaissance made for rear positions for M.G.'s, those previously selected involving too much labour. New positions selected for 8 guns in POMPADOUR. Report of this sent to Bde. Strength. 2nd Lt. T.C. BENNETT proceeded to join 75th M.G. Coy by order of Reserve Army. No. 21279 Sergt. JONES slightly wounded by shell hitting Sap 2 gun emplacement.	
"	July 24th		87th M.G. Coy (less 3 officers + 37 men) relieved from trenches by 74th M.G. Coy, & marched to BUS where night was spent in huts. 3 officers + 37 men were left behind in the trenches for 1 day to help incoming Company.	
BUS	July 25th		87th M.G.Coy less 3 officers + 37 men (rearguard party) marched from BUS to AMPLIER, arriving 1 p.m. Billets in huts. Rearguard party marched from ENGLEBELMER direct to AMPLIER arriving 8 p.m.	
AMPLIER	July 26th		Coy. Operation Order No. 6 issued re entraining & move to PROVEN	See App. 4.

Army Form C. 2118

WAR DIARY
or
INTELLIGENCE SUMMARY
(Erase heading not required.)

Place	Date	Hour	Summary of Events and Information	Remarks and references to Appendices
AMPLIER	July 27th		87th M.G. Coy moved by train to PROVEN, No. 1 section at 12 noon with 2nd S.W.B.	
			— 2 — 3.15 p.m. — 1st K.O.S.B.	
			— 3 — 6.15 p.m. — 1st R. Innis: Fus.	
			— 4 — 9.15 p.m. — 1st Border Regt.	see App 5.
PROVEN	July 30		Special Order of the Day issued.	
			Reconnaissance of trenches in YPRES salient by C.O. and 5 officers.	
PROVEN	July 31		87th M.G. Coy relieved 71st M.G. Coy in the trenches (YPRES SALIENT) Coy proceeded by train to YPRES at 8.30 p.m., relief being completed about midnight. Transport proceeded by road to transport lines close to VLAMERTINGHE.	

Place	Date	Hour	Summary of Events and Information	Remarks and references to Appendices
PROVEN	July 30th		Remarks.	

Employment.

Owing to the systematic shelling of trenches prior to an attack, it is strongly felt that the efficiency of the Defence rests on deep dug-outs rather than on M.G. emplacements.

It is essential that the guns can be brought into action quickly, & certain guns should remain in concrete or steel rail emplacements to check any advance until the guns in deep dug-outs are in action.

Establishment.

(1.) Officers. A Transport Officer is found necessary owing to the amount of transport with each Coy. The 2/C in command cannot do the duty of Transport Officer owing to the amount of Orderly Room work.

(2.) Signallers. The signalling personnel & equipment is not sufficient. It is recommended that 18 Signallers & 9 telephones be the establishment.

(3.) Orderly Room. No personnel available for Orderly Room Clerks. At least 2 clerks are required.

WAR DIARY
or
INTELLIGENCE SUMMARY

Army Form C. 2118

Place	Date	Hour	Summary of Events and Information	Remarks and references to Appendices
PROVEN	July 31		(4) Casualties. The personnel should be 200. There are no men available for replacing casualties. This leads to guns getting out of action. (5) Transport. A travelling Kitchen for the Machine Gun Coy is urgently required. This is particularly so when troops are on the march. J.H.R. Burrill Capt Comdg 87th M.S. Coy.	

Appendix I

List of Casualties in Action on July 1st 1916

87th Bde Machine Gun Company

Killed.
Officers —
Other Ranks 3

Missing believed Killed.
Officers { Lt. E.W. COSTELLO
2Lt. T.F. BREENE.
Other Ranks 3

Missing.
Officers —
Other Ranks 4

Wounded.
Officers —
Other Ranks 11.

Died of Wounds.
Officers —
Other Ranks 1.

Appendix 2

MESSAGE.

From
Lieut.-General SIR AYLMER HUNTER-WESTON, K.C.B., D.S.O.
To
All OFFICERS, N.C.O.'s and MEN of the VIII. Army Corps.

In so big a command as an Army Corps of four Divisions (about eighty thousand men) it is impossible for me to come round all front line trenches and all billets to see every man as I wish to do. You must take the will for the deed, and accept this printed message in place of the spoken word.

It is difficult for me to express my admiration for the splendid courage, determination and discipline displayed by every Officer, N.C.O. and Man of the Battalions that took part in the great attack on the BEAUMONT-HAMEL-SERRE position on the 1st July. All observers agree in stating that the various waves of men issued from their trenches and moved forward at the appointed time in perfect order, undismayed by the heavy artillery fire and deadly machine gun fire. There were no cowards nor waverers, and not a man fell out. It was a magnificent display of disciplined courage worthy of the best traditions of the British race.

Very few are left of my old comrades, the original "Contemptibles," but their successors in the 4th Division have shewn that they are worthy to bear the honours gained by the 4th Division at their first great fight at Fontaine-au-Pire and Ligny, during the great Retreat and greater Advance across the Marne and Aisne, and in all the hard fighting at Ploegsteert and at Ypres.

Though but few of my old comrades, the heroes of the historic landing at Cape Helles, are still with us, the 29th Division of to-day has shown itself capable of maintaining its high traditions, and has proved itself worthy of its hard earned title of "The Incomparable 29th."

The 31st New Army Division, and the 48th Territorial Division, by the heroism and discipline of the units engaged in this their first big battle, have proved themselves worthy to fight by the side of such magnificent regular Divisions as the 4th and 29th. There can be no higher praise.

We had the most difficult part of the line to attack. The Germans had fortified it with skill and immense labour for many months, they had kept their best troops here, and had assembled North, East, and South-East of it a formidable collection of artillery and many machine guns.

By your splendid attack you held these enemy forces here in the North and so enabled our friends in the South, both British and French, to achieve the brilliant success that they have. Therefore, though we did not do all we hoped to do you have more than pulled your weight, and you and our even more glorious comrades who have preceded us across the Great Divide have nobly done your Duty.

We have got to stick it out and go on hammering. Next time we attack, if it please God, we will not only pull our weight but will pull off a big thing. With such troops as you, who are determined to stick it out and do your duty, we are certain of winning through to a glorious victory.

I salute each Officer, N.C.O. and Man of the 4th, 29th, 31st, and 48th Divisions as a comrade-in-arms and I rejoice to have the privilege of commanding such a band of heroes as the VIII. Corps have proved themselves to be.

H.Q., VIII. CORPS,
4th July, 1916.

AYLMER HUNTER-WESTON.
Lieut.-General.

ARMY PRINTING AND STATIONERY SERVICES A. 7/16 80,000.

Appendix 3.

SPECIAL ORDER OF THE DAY
BY
GENERAL SIR DOUGLAS HAIG,
G.C.B., K.C.I.E., K.C.V.O., A.D.C.
Commander-in-Chief, British Armies in France.

The following telegrams, sent on the occasion of the celebration of the French National Fête on July 14th, are published for the information of all ranks:—

I. MONSIEUR POINCARÉ, PRESIDENT OF THE FRENCH REPUBLIC.

14th July.

The British Army, fighting by the side of the brave soldiers of France in the bitter struggle now proceeding, expresses on the occasion of this great anniversary its admiration for the results achieved by the French Army and its unshakeable confidence in the speedy realization of our common hopes.

SIR DOUGLAS HAIG.

II. GENERAL SIR D. HAIG, COMMANDER-IN-CHIEF, BRITISH ARMIES IN FRANCE.

14th July.

I thank you, my dear General, for the good wishes which you have expressed towards France, and beg you to convey to the brave British Army my lively admiration of the fine successes which it has just achieved and which only this morning have been so brilliantly extended. They have produced a deep impression on the hearts of all Frenchmen. Those of your magnificent troops who have to-day paraded in the streets of Paris, in company with those of our Allies, received throughout their march a striking proof of the public sentiment. I am glad to have this opportunity of sending you—to you personally and to your troops—my warm congratulations.

POINCARÉ.

D. Haig, Genl.

Commanding-in-Chief,
British Armies in France

General Headquarters,
18th July, 1916.

87th Brigade Machine Gun Coy
Operations Order No 6 Dated July 26th 1916

I. On the 27th inst the Company will entrain at DOULLENS SOUTH and proceed to HAZEBROUCK.

II. Troops will accompany Transport for loading purposes and march via RUE DE BOURS, RUE DE TRIBUNAL, and AVENUE DE LA GARE, to the RUE des NEUF MOULINS. Where they will halt until required to entrain.

III. The train journey will probably occupy 8 hours all horses should therefore be watered prior to leaving their Bivouacs.

IV. The Company will detrain at PROVEN unless notified on arrival at HAZEBROUCK.

V. The Company will be accomodated at POPERINGHE.

VI. Train time table attached.

VII. Officers I/c Sections will report to O.C. Coy before 6 pm today to Reconnoitre the Route.

VIII. Baggage will accompany Coys Transport and arrive 3 hours before the time of Departure of their train.

IX. One days Rations will be carried on the Man.

X. The following Serial Number allotted to 87th Bde M.G. Coy 2926

No 1 Copy to Office
" 2 & 9 " " War Diary
" 3   " " 87th Brigade
" 4   " " Lieut Green R.E.
" 5   " " Jenkins
" 6   " " Hunter
" 7   " " Outwin
" 8   " " Ledwood

Capt O.C. 87 Bde M.G. Coy

Train Time Table

Load Sent forward	Train Number	Unit attacked	Time of Departure
No 1 Section 81 Bde M.G. Coy / 3 Limbered Wagon / 1 Water Cart / 4 Officers Chargers + all spare animals / Head Quarters	2926	2nd S.L.B. (2921)	12.19
No 2 Section 81st M.G. Coy / 3 Limbered Wagon / 1 Officers Charger	2926	1st K.O.S.B. (2922)	15.34
No 3 Section 81st M.G. Coy / 3 Limbered Wagon / 1 G.S. Wagon / 1 Officers Charger	2926	1 R. Innis. Fus. (2923)	18.19
No 4 Section 81st M.G. Coy / 3 Limbered Wagon / 3 Officers Chargers	2926	1st Border Regt (2924)	21.19

Appendix 5.

SPECIAL ORDER OF THE DAY

BY

GENERAL SIR DOUGLAS HAIG,
G.C.B., K.C.I.E., K.C.V.O., A.D.C.
Commander-in-Chief, British Armies in France.

The following telegrams, sent on the occasion of the celebration of the Belgian National Fête, are published for information:—

I. HIS MAJESTY THE KING OF THE BELGIANS.

July 21st.

On the occasion of this great anniversary I respectfully beg on behalf of the British Army under my command to offer to Your Majesty and the Belgian nation the expression of our admiration and sympathy. Fighting as we are side by side with your gallant soldiers for the same ideal we feel thoroughly confident that by the united efforts of all the Allies victory cannot fail at no distant date to be ours.

DOUGLAS HAIG.

II. GENERAL SIR D. HAIG.

July 22nd.

I thank you heartily for the good wishes you send me on behalf of the British Army and I express you my sincere admiration for the great bravery displayed by your gallant troops.

ALBERT.

General Headquarters,
27th July, 1916.

Commanding-in-Chief,
British Armies in France.

ARMY PRINTING AND STATIONERY SERVICES A—7/16

29th Division.

87th Infantry Brigade.

87th MACHINE GUN COMPany

AUGUST 1916

CONFIDENTIAL.

WAR DIARY

of

87th Machine Gun Company

From August 1st 1916 To August 31st 1916.

(Volume 3.)

Army Form C. 2118

Instructions regarding War Diaries and Intelligence Summaries are contained in F. S. Regs., Part II. and the Staff Manual respectively. Title Pages will be prepared in manuscript.

WAR DIARY
or
INTELLIGENCE SUMMARY
(Erase heading not required.)

Place	Date	Hour	Summary of Events and Information	Remarks and references to Appendices
YPRES	August 2nd		1 O.R. evacuated SICK & struck off strength of Company	
"		4 p.	Fighting strength of Coy :- 8 officers. 132 O.R.	
"		5 p.	No 3 Section relieved by No 2 Section.	
"		7 p.	'Gas Alarm' orders owing to change in direction of wind	
"		8 p.	Gas Alarm sounded at about 10.15 p.m. The gas cloud sent over by Germans was mostly on our right, & only affected the 3 gun teams in the POTIJZE group. These were all given absolute protection by the use of P.H.G. helmets & Box Respirators. Slow rate of fire maintained during Gas Discharge. Guns not officers except for slight corrosion afterwards. Relief of Coy by 86th N.9 Coy arranged for 10 p.m. Transport were therefore in YPRES when gas cloud came over. Animals not seriously affected. Probably only outskirts of gas cloud reached them - Relief not completed till 4 a.m. 9/10. 2 officers and 11 O.R. left in trenches for 24 hours to assist incoming unit. Casualties: 2/Lt. S.G. OUTWIN wounded slightly, at duty. 1 O.R. wounded slightly (by gas).	
BRANDHOEK	9th		Company proceeded to Machine Gun rest camp at BRANDHOEK. 8 men from each Btn. in the Bde attached to the Company as a permanent working party.	

Army Form C. 2118

WAR DIARY
or
INTELLIGENCE SUMMARY
(Erase heading not required.)

Instructions regarding War Diaries and Intelligence Summaries are contained in F. S. Regs., Part II. and the Staff Manual respectively. Title Pages will be prepared in manuscript.

Place	Date	Hour	Summary of Events and Information	Remarks and references to Appendices
BRANDHOEK	14th		About 11 p.m. gas alarm sounded. Coy stood to with helmets & respirators for about 30 minutes, till it was discovered to be a false alarm.	
"	15th		No 21418 Pte J. COLLINS awarded Military Medal for gallant conduct on July 1st 1916. 2 O.R. taken on strength of Coy.	
"	16th		About 4 A.M. gas alarm sounded. Coy stood to for about 3/4 of an hour, till it was discovered to be a false alarm. (NB. The wind was blowing in the wrong direction.)	
"	17th		1 O.R. taken on strength of Coy from Base Depot.	
"	18th		Coy relieved 86th M.G. Coy in the line, in left sector.	
YPRES	19th		1 O.R. evacuated to M.G. Corps Base Depot, under-age.	
"	20th		2 gas alarms sounded, one about 9pm, the other about 11pm. Both were false alarms.	
"	22nd		The M.G. in WIELTJE ESTAMINET was temporarily moved back to a position in Bn Trench, owing to the ESTAMINET getting about 6 direct hits from German Field Guns.	
"	23rd		1 NR. evacuated Sick out of Divl Area. No 2 Section moved to POTIJZE group. WIELTJE group. No 1 Section No 3 & 4 Sections remained at ST JEAN.	

WAR DIARY
or
INTELLIGENCE SUMMARY
(Erase heading not required.)

Army Form C. 2118

Place	Date	Hour	Summary of Events and Information	Remarks and references to Appendices
YPRES	23."		From this date the 4 guns at Coy H.Q. QM became part of Divisional Reserve. In event of heavy enemy attack they had orders to man 4 positions on the RAMPARTS – KARTE SALIENT line – The M.G. Coy at rest at BRANDHOEK became Corps Reserve.	
"	28."		As a result of this it was decided to bring one complete section to Coy H.Q., instead of 1 gun from each section as previously. No.1 gun from each section for covering the North side of WIELTJE was allotted to B/2 Trench M.G. position at C.28.a.45.80. It was proposed to erect a concrete emplacement here – No.3 Section became Divisional Reserve at Coy H.Q., No.2 Section remains at POTIJZE, No.1 Section went to ST JEAN, & No.4 Section to WIELTJE.	
"	29."		Gas attack on German lines arranged on 87th Bde front. Out of 11 M.G's in [ ] Bde front. line 9 were to open rapid fire on German front line system & communication trenches 10 minutes after commencement of gas discharge – Fire was to continue for 40 minutes & then cease for 1 hour; then another 10 minute burst; then fire at irregular intervals from dawn till 6.30 AM. Arrangements made with M.G. Coys on right & left to fire on German front lines opposite our front, while we fired on their front –	

1875 Wt. W593/826 1,000,000 4/15 J.B.C. & A. A.D.S.S./Forms/C. 2118.

Army Form C. 2118

WAR DIARY
or
INTELLIGENCE SUMMARY
(Erase heading not required.)

Instructions regarding War Diaries and Intelligence Summaries are contained in F. S. Regs., Part II. and the Staff Manual respectively. Title Pages will be prepared in manuscript.

Place	Date	Hour	Summary of Events and Information	Remarks and references to Appendices
YPRES	29th		Gas Discharge was timed for 1.30 A.M. Owing to unfavourable wind, operations were postponed for the night at about 9 p.m.	
"	30th		False alarm of gas about 11 p.m. Same night operations arranged as for previous night. Again postponed owing to unfavourable wind.	
"	31st		Same operations arranged as for previous night. Again postponed owing to unfavourable wind. General Average of about 8,000 rounds has been fired nightly on German roads, trench tramways, communication trenches etc. Aeroplane emplacement has also been constructed for firing by day on hostile aircraft. About 25 men have been employed nightly in assisting R.E.'s in construction of a large double loophole concrete emplacement in disused trench at C.28.d.2.3. Fighting strength of Coy. on 31.7.16 :- 8 Officers - 142 Other Ranks.	

J.H.R. Benwell
Capt.
Comm'd 87th Machine Gun Coy

29th Division.

87th Infantry Brigade.

87th MACHINE GUN COMPANY

SEPTEMBER 1 9 1 6

CONFIDENTIAL

WAR DIARY

of

87th Machine Gun Company

From September 1st to September 30th 1916

Volume 4.

WAR DIARY
INTELLIGENCE SUMMARY

Army Form C. 2118

Place	Date	Hour	Summary of Events and Information	Remarks and references to Appendices
YPRES	1st		Same night operations arranged as for previous night. Again postponed owing to unfavourable wind. Casualties 2 O.R. wounded (1 slightly, at duty.)	
	2nd		Night operations again postponed. Casualty 1 O.R. Killed (self-inflicted) Relief between sections took place as follows:— No 1 to POTIJZE group — 2 — Coy H.Q. — 3 — WIELTJE group — 4 — ST JEAN group	
	3rd 4th		Gas alarm at about 11 p.m., again at 2 A.m. (3-9-16) Both false alarms. Court of Inquiry held into death of No 21300 Pte Davies. 1 O.R. evacuated sick out of Divl Area.	
	5th		New M.G. position decided on about 130 yards north of WIELTJE ESTAMINET in old shell craters for covering ADMIRAL'S ROAD & East of WIELTJE. New M.G. position started in front of B 12 trench to fire East, covering WIELTJE.	
	7th		1 O.R. evacuated sick out of Divisional Area.	
	8th		Coy relieved by 56th M.G. Coy & proceeded to rest camp at BRANDHOEK.	

WAR DIARY or INTELLIGENCE SUMMARY

Army Form C. 2118

(Erase heading not required.)

Instructions regarding War Diaries and Intelligence Summaries are contained in F.S. Regs., Part II. and the Staff Manual respectively. Title Pages will be prepared in manuscript.

Place	Date	Hour	Summary of Events and Information	Remarks and references to Appendices
BRANDHOEK	11th		2/Lt C.H. PAYNE taken in strength of Company.	
"	16th		Fighting strength of Company: 9 Officers. 139 Other Ranks.	
YPRES	18th		Company relieved 86th M.G. Coy in the left sector, Nos 1, 3, 4 sections going into the line, No. 2 Section being in Divisional Reserve at Coy H.Q. List of M.G. targets issues for ensuing week. Section relief in the line as follows:— No. 1 Section & Coy H.Q. (Divisional Reserve) — WIELTJE group, 2 — ST JEAN, 3 — ST JEAN, 4 — POTIJZE	See App. 1.
"	23rd			
"	24th		1 O.R. wounded slightly, at duty.	
"	25th		Anti Aircraft emplacement erected at ST JEAN, to be manned by day by the team of 6 F gun. List of M.G. targets issued for ensuing week.	See App. 2.
"	26th		2 O.R. evacuated sick out of Divisional Area.	

WAR DIARY or INTELLIGENCE SUMMARY

Army Form C. 2118

Place	Date	Hour	Summary of Events and Information	Remarks and references to Appendices
YPRES	28th		Section Relief in the line as follows:— No 1 Section to WIELTJE group — 2 — ST JEAN — 3 — POTIJZE — 4 — Coy H.Q. (Div² Reserve)	
"	29th		2 O.R. evacuated sick out of Divisional Area.	
"	30th		Raid undertaken by 1st BORDER Regt. on German trenches opposite WIELTJE — 87th Machine Gun Coy co-operated. 87th M.G. Coy Operation Order N° 6 issued — Ammunition expenditure during night: 20,650 rounds.	See App. 3.

A R Bunnill
Major

Appendix I

	Sept. 19th	Sept. 20th	Sept. 21st	Sept. 22nd	Sept. 23rd	Sept. 24th	Sept. 25th
PROWSE FARM gun.	1.) C18C1.0. to SQUARE FARM 8–9 11–12.30	1.) ST JULIEN Rd. C17 & 8.5 to VANHEULE FARM. 8–9 10.30–11 4–5 5.30–6	1.) Trench Tramway from C27 & 5.3 to C24 d 4.2 11–12 3–5	As for Sept. 21st	As for Sept. 20th	As for Sept. 19th	ST JULIEN Rd. C17 & 8.5 to VANHEULE FARM. 9–10.30 12.30–2 3–3.40 4–6
	2.) ST JULIEN ROAD C17 & 8.5 to VANHEULE FARM. 1.30–3 4–5.30	2.) BANK FARM to SPREE FARM. (Tramway) 8–4 10–10.30 12–1 2–3	2.) C18C10 to SQUARE FARM 8–4 10–10.30				
X4 gun.	1.) ZONNEBEKE Road, d. Tramway running from BIRR CROSSROADS to d. Tramway 8.30–10 2–4	1.) Communication trench running from BULL COTTAGE RUIN to C8 a 2.7. 11–12 1–2	1.) Tramway from GREY RUIN to C8 a 2.7. 11–12 1–2	As for Sept. 21st	As for Sept. 20th	As for Sept. 19th	Tramway from C24 d 6.2 to ZONNEBEKE Road. 8–10 12–1 2–3.30 4.30–6
	2.) Tramway from C24 & 8.3 to ZONNEBEKE Road. 11–12 12.30–1.30	2.) ZONNEBEKE Rd & Road. 8.30–10.30 4.30–6	2.) Tramway from C24 & 8.3 to ZONNEBEKE Road. 8–9 9.30–10.30 3–4 5–6				
4.5 gun.	1.) ST JULIEN Road from C17 & 8.5 to VANHEULE FARM. 12–1.30 2–2.30	1.) Sand road from SPREE FARM to RAT FARM. 8–9 9.30–10 11–12 2–3	1.) ST JULIEN Road from C17 & 6.5 to VANHEULE FARM. 8.30–10 11.30–1 2.30–4 5–6	As for Sept. 21st	As for Sept. 20th	As for Sept. 19th	ST JULIEN Rd. 8–9.30 10.30–12 2–3 3.30–4.30 5–6
	2.) ST JULIEN Road from C17 & 8.5 to VANHEULE FARM. 4.30–6	2.) ST JULIEN Rd. 4.30–6					

Sept. 19th	Sept. 20th	Sept. 21st	Sept. 22nd	Sept. 23rd	Sept. 24th	Sept. 25th	Sept. 26th
1.) ST JULIEN Rd. from Fork C.23.a.5.2. to CHEDDAR VILLA.	1.) Traverse from C.16.d.3.1. to VON HÜGEL FARM.	As for Sept. 19th.	As for Sept. 19th.	As for Sept. 20th.	As for Sept. 20th.		
8.30 – 9.30 10 – 10.30 2.30 – 3.30 4.30 – 5.30	8 – 8.30 9 – 10 11 – 11.45 3 – 3.30 4 – 4.30 5.15 – 6						
2.) Traverse from C.16.d.4.2. to VON HÜGEL FARM.	2.) ST JULIEN Rd						
11 – 11.30 12 – 12.30 1 – 2	12.30 – 1.30 2 – 2.30						
3.) Traverse from X roads C.29.c.9.6. to C.29.c.5.3., also along road from VON HÜGEL FM. to UHLAN FM.	3.) Traverse from X roads C.23.c.9.6. to C.29.c.5.3., also along road from VON HÜGEL FM to UHLAN FM.	As for Sept. 20th	As for Sept. 19th	As for Sept. 19th	As for Sept. 19th		
8.30 – 10 11 – 12 2.15 – 2.45 3.30 – 4.15 5 – 5.30	8 – 8.45 9 – 9.30 10.15 – 10.30 11 – 12.30 1.30 – 3 3.45 – 4 4.15 – 5						
4.) Communication Trench leading to APPLE VILLA.	4.) Communication Trench leading to PLUM FARM.						
12.30 – 1.30	1 – 2						

Appendix II

	Sept 26th	Sept 27th	Sept 28th	Sept 29th	Sept 30th	Oct 1st	Oct 2nd
Patrol	1) St. Julien Road C.17.b.5. to Vanheule Farm 7.30 – 9 9.30 – 12 5 – 6 2) Search Trenches from C.29.b.5.2 to C.24.a.9.7 10.30 – 12 1 – 3 4 – 6	1) Bank Farm to Spree Farm (Trenches) 7.45 – 9 9.30 – 11 5 – 6 2) St. Julien Road C.17.b.5. to Vanheule Farm 10 – 12 1 – 3 3 – 4	1) St. Julien Road C.17.b.5. to Vanheule Farm 9 – 9.30 10 – 11 5 – 6 2) Zonnebeke Road Br. Trench alongside 9 – 9.30 10.45 – 12 1 – 2 3) Grey Ruin C.30.b.2.7. 3.30 – 5 5.40 – 6	1) C.18.C.1.0 to Square Farm (Trench) 8.30 – 10.30 12 – 1.30 2 – 3 4 – 6 2) Trenches from C.24.d.8.3 to Zonnebeke Road 8 – 10 11 – 12 1 – 2.30 3.30 – 5 5.30 – 6	As for Sept 27th As for Sept 26th As for Sept 28th	As for Sept 26 As for Sept 29th "Search" from Spree Farm to Rat Farm 8 – 9.30 10 – 11 5 – 6	As for Sept 27th As for Sept 27th 1) St. Julien Road C.17.b.5. to Vanheule Farm 12 – 1 2 – 4
	3) Zonnebeke Road Br. Trench alongside Siu Cottage 7.30 – 8.30 9.45 – 11 1.30 – 2 4) St. Julien Road from C.17.b.6.6 to Vanheule Farm from C.17.b.8.5 to Vanheule Farm 7.30 – 8.30 10.30 – 11.30 5) "Search" from Rat Farm Spree Farm 11.30 – 1.30 3.45 – 5 5 – 6	3) Zonnebeke Road Br. Trench alongside 4) St. Julien Road C.17.b.8.5 to Vanheule Farm 7.30 – 8 10 – 10.30 11.30 – 1 2 – 3 4 – 6 5) Search from Spree Farm to Rat Farm 9 – 9.30 10.30 – 12 0.30 – 3 4 – 6					

	Sept 26th	Sept 27th	Sept 28th	Sept 29th	Sept 30th	Oct 1st	Oct 2
8G	Traverse from C.16.c.4.2. to VON HUGEL FARM 7.30 - 8.30 10 - 11.30 1 - 2 3 - 5 5.45 - 6	ST. JULIEN ROAD from Fork C.23.a.5.2. TO CHEDDAR VILLA 7.45 - 9 10.30 - 12 1.30 - 3 4.30 - 6	1) ST JULIEN ROAD C.23.a.5.2. TO CHEDDAR VILLA 7.30 - 8.30 10 - 11 5 - 6 2) Traverse from C.16.d.4.2. TO VON HUGEL FARM 12 - 1.30 2.30 - 4	As for 28th	As For 26th	As for Sept 27	As for Sept 28th
WALK GUN	Traverse from X ROAD C.23.c.9.6. TO C.29.b.5.3. also along road from VON HUGEL FARM TO UHLAN FARM 8 - 10 11.30 - 1 2 - 3.30 5 - 6	1) "Communn" Trench leading to PLUM FARM 8 - 9 10 - 11 2) Traverse from X ROAD C.23.c.9.6. TO C.29.b.5.3. also along road from VON HUGEL FARM TO UHLAN FARM 12.30 - 2 3 - 4.30 5.30 - 6.	1) "Traverse from X ROAD C.23.c.9.6. TO C.29.b.5.3. also along road from VON HUGEL FARM TO UHLAN FARM 7.30 - 9 9.30 - 10.30 12 - 1 2 - 3.30 2) Communn Trench leading to APPLE VILLA 4.30 - 6.	As For 27	As For 28th	As for Sept 26th	

G. H. Moberley J.P.
Lieut. & Gunley
67th Machine Gunley

87th Machine Gun Company Operation Order No 8

Appendix III

A. 1) A raid will be carried out by the 1st Border Regt on the night of Sept. 30th
Point of Entry C.29.a.30.95
The 87th Machine Gun Company will co-operate.

2) **Fire Table**

1930 — M.G's at 4.C. 8.0. and NEW PROWSE emplacement open fire

2030 — Artillery opens fire also M.G's at LA BRIQUE B.A. B.C. and CONGREVE WALK.

2050 — M.G's at PROWSE FARM. X.4. and 4.A. open fire

2055 — All Artillery lifts to 2nd line.
Party enters German trenches
On completion of task, or by 2125 party will withdraw

2150 — All Artillery and Machine Guns cease fire.

2300 – 2330 }
0045 – 0115 } 10 M.G's as already detailed open fire again on
0230 – 0330 } same targets.
0415 – 0530 } (NOTE Artillery will open fire again about 2300)

B. **Machine Gun Targets**

Machine Guns will fire as follows:-

PROWSE F^m & X.4. — Traverse from C.29.b.0.0. to C.29.b.6.2.

CONGREVE WALK — Search Communⁿ trenches to APPLE VILLA & PLUM FARM.

4.A. Traverse from C.23.a.1.6. to C.23.c.9.6.

4.C. Search ST. JULIEN ROAD from WELL COTTAGE to CHEDDAR VILLA

B.C. Search FORTUIN ROAD from C.23.c.6.2. to C.23.b.8.1.

NEW PROWSE FARM Search ZONNEBEKE ROAD.

B.D. Traverse from C.29.d.9.3. to I.0.a.2.6.

LA BRIQUE Traverse German front line between BELLE VIEW & WELL COTTAGE

B.A. Search ST JULIEN ROAD from C.23.d.0.0. to C.23.c.3.3.

Sept. 30th 1916.

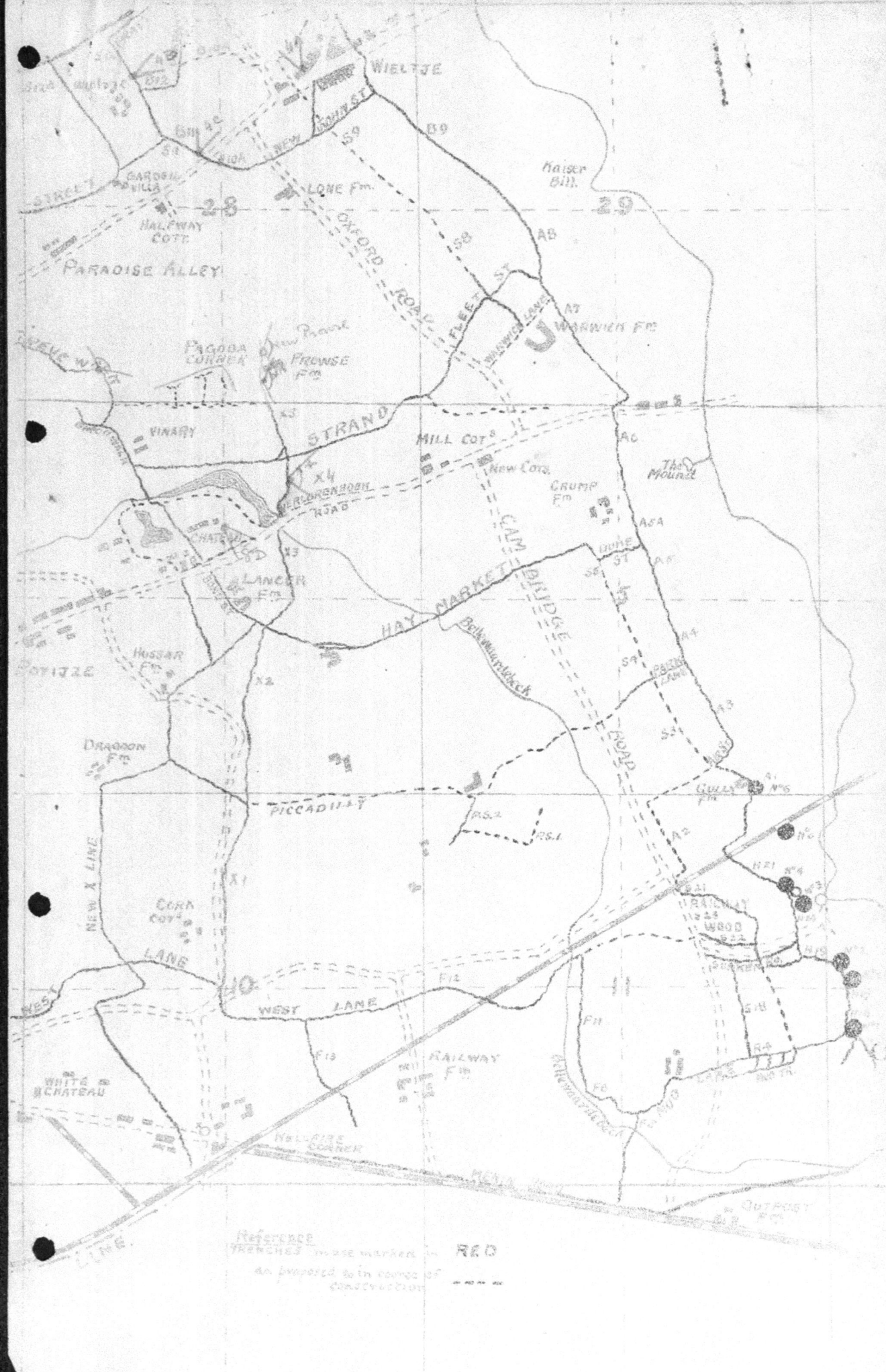

29th Division.

87th Infantry Brigade.

87th MACHINE GUN COMPANY

OCTOBER 1 9 1 6

CONFIDENTIAL.

WAR DIARY
of
87th Machine Gun Company

From October 1st 1916 To October 31st 1916.

(VOLUME 5)

Army Form C. 2118

WAR DIARY
INTELLIGENCE SUMMARY
(Erase heading not required.)

Instructions regarding War Diaries and Intelligence Summaries are contained in F. S. Regs, Part II. and the Staff Manual respectively. Title Pages will be prepared in manuscript.

Place	Date	Hour	Summary of Events and Information	Remarks and references to Appendices
YPRES	3rd		Company relieved from Trenches by 166th M.G. Coy, & proceeded to 'J' Camp. 1 O.R. taken on strength of Coy.	
'J' Camp	7th		Company marched off from 'J' camp to PROVEN, where they entrained for SALEUX. Coy arrives SALEUX about 11 p.m., & marched to ALLONVILLE	
ALLONVILLE	8th		2/Lieut G.S.T. DOWNES taken on Strength of Company, also 1 other Rank.	
"	9th		5 O.R. taken on strength of Company. 2 O.R. evacuated sick out of Area.	
"	10th		Company marched from ALLONVILLE to BUIRE, where they went into Billets. 1 O.R. evacuated sick out of Area 1 O.R. evacuated to base for Munition work in England	
BUIRE	14th		Company marched by road to FRICOURT Camp. 2/Lt. W.H. LEWIN & 1 O.R. taken on strength of Company.	
FRICOURT	18th		Orders received for Company to be ready to march off at 2 hours notice Trenches occupied by 89th Bde (on left on FLERS) reconnoitred with a view to taking over on evening of 18th inst. Relief cancelled. Orders received to be in readiness to relieve 88th M.G. Coy in trenches on night of FLERS.	

1875 Wt. W593/826 1,000,000 4/15 J.B.C. & A. A.D.S.S./Forms/C. 2118.

WAR DIARY
INTELLIGENCE SUMMARY
(Erase heading not required.)

Army Form C. 2118

Place	Date	Hour	Summary of Events and Information	Remarks and references to Appendices
FRICOURT	19th		At 11.30 am Company with Transport marched to BERNAFAY WOOD Camp. Owing to congestion in roads this was only reached at dusk.	
BERNAFAY	20th	1.30 p.m	Company proceeded to the trenches to relieve 88th M.G. Coy. (Coy Operation Order No 9 issued). Owing to blocking of Traffic on roads, gun limbers did not arrive. Nos 1 & 3 sections proceeded to front line (GREASE TRENCH) arriving there at 5 am the following morning. Remainder proceeding forthwith owing to non-arrival of limbers. {1 Offr wounded in action {1 OR. evacuated sick out of Divl. Area.	See App. I
Trenches	21st		Relief proceeded with. No 2 Section proceeded to HILT TRENCH (in support) - No 4 Section to GIRD TRENCH (in reserve) Coy H.Q. established at S12 b 5.7. (Reffe map Sheet No: 57 a SW) Trenches reconnoitred with a view to selecting positions from which to support an attack.	

WAR DIARY
INTELLIGENCE SUMMARY
(Erase heading not required.)

Army Form C. 2118

Place	Date	Hour	Summary of Events and Information	Remarks and references to Appendices
Trenches	22nd		Nos 2 & 4 Sections relieved Nos 1 & 3 in GREASE & HILT TRENCHES, the latter going back to GIRD TRENCH. 2 O.R. killed in action.	
"	23rd		Attack by 13th on our right endangered trenches; supported by Nos 1 & 3 sections from GIRD TRENCH. 2 O.R. wounded in action.	See App. 2.
			Coy. Operation Order No 10 issued. 2/Lt. S.G. OUTWIN wounded in action. 2 O.R. evacuated sick out of area.	
			Operations for 28th inst. postponed till 28th.	
"	24th		1 O.R. killed in action. 3 O.R. wounded in action.	
"	25th		Nos 1 & 3 sections relieved Nos 2 & 4 in GREASE TRENCH & HILT TRENCH. Nos 2 & 4 going back to GIRD TRENCH.	
			One of the 4 guns in HILT TRENCH was moved to new communication trench (PETROL LANE) at N.20.d.5.4., before along the valley northwards.	
"	26th		Operations again postponed from 28th to 30th inst.	
"	28th		Company Operation Order No 11 issued. (Operations again postponed for 48 hours, i.e. from Oct. 30th to Nov. 1st.)	See App. 13.

WAR DIARY
INTELLIGENCE SUMMARY

(Erase heading not required.)

Army Form C. 2118.

Place	Date	Hour	Summary of Events and Information	Remarks and references to Appendices
Trenches	29th		Company relieved from the Trenches by 2nd Australian M.G. Coy. Owing to congested state of the trenches, relief not completed till following morning.	
"	30th		Company marched to POMMIERS CAMP, from thence to FRICOURT Camp. 6 O.R. taken on strength of Coy.	
FRICOURT	31st		Lt. M.G.M.C. RANDALL, and 2/Lt. L.K. MORRIS taken on strength of Coy from CAMIERS.	

H.R. Burnill
Major
Commdg. 89th Machine Gun Coy

SECRET

87th Machine Gun Company.
Operation Order No 9.

Appendix I

In the Field
Oct 20th 1916

1) The 87th Infantry Bde will relieve the 88th Infty Bde in the right sector extending from N 21 d 07 to N 20 c 81 on the nights of 19th/20th and 20th/21st Oct. 1916

2) 87th M.G. Coy will relieve 88th M.G. Coy at 3 pm to-day. The Coy will parade ready to march off at 1 pm. Transport will leave Transport Lines not later than 12 noon & will move independently to arrive at Coy H.Q. at S 12 b 6 8 at 3 pm. Lt Hunter will act as guide.

Nos 1 & 3 Sections will proceed to the front line (GREASE TRENCH) No 2 Section to HILT TRENCH, & No 4 Section to GIRD TRENCH (in reserve)

3) Water bottles will be filled – Rations for 21st inst will be cooked to-day & carried in the haversack.

4) All picks & shovels will be taken to Coy. H.Q.

5) Each team will be composed of 1 NCO, 3 gunners & 1 attached man.
In addition Nos 3 & 4 Sections will take up 1 runner per section

6) The following will be taken up with each gun team :— Gun, spare parts, 1 tin of water for gun — 2 tins of water for drinking — 2 "Tommies Cookers" — 1 Primus Stove with paraffin. Tripods & belt boxes will be taken over from 88th M.G. Coy.

7) Officers will send down a list to Coy H.Q. with relieved team, of exactly what has been taken over from 88th M.G. Coy.

8) All men not required for gun teams (as detailed in para. 5.) will proceed to Transport Lines

9) Coy Transport will remain where they are at present

J H Mobert.
Lieut & Adjt
87th M.G. Coy

87th Machine Gun Company.
Operation Order No 9 Copy No
Appendix II

1) The 87th Brigade will attack the enemy's line on the 25th inst. at an hour to be notified later (called "zero"). The 86th Brigade on our left & the Brigade on our right are also attacking.

2) The Brigade objective is to dig in on a line from cross roads at N 21 b 9 4 to N 15 c 3 4 — 1st Border Regt will be on the left & the 1st KOSB on the right.

3) 2 Machine Guns from No 4 Section under 2nd Lieut Downes will be attached to 1st Border Regt.
   2 Machine Guns from No 2 Section under 2nd Lieut Farrant will be attached to 1st KOSB Regt.
   2 Machine Guns from No 4 Section under 2nd Lieut. Hunter will act as a Mobile Section on the left flank & will reinforce the 1st Border Regt as soon as possible after the new position has been consolidated.
   2 Machine Guns from No 2 Section under 2nd Lt Lewin will act as a mobile Section on the right flank & will reinforce the 1st KOSB Regt as soon as possible after the new position has been consolidated.
   2nd Lt Downes & Hunter will report to OC 1st Border Regt & 2nd Lt Farrant & Lewin to 1st KOSB Regt before 12 noon on 24th inst. for instructions.

4) No 3 Section will take up positions to be fixed later.
   No 1 Section will take up positions in GIRD TRENCH.
   These sections will support the attack with overhead fire particular attention being paid to BARLEY TRENCH.

5) 1st Border Regt will detail 10 men as carriers for 2nd Lt Downes & 6 men as carriers for 2 Lt Hunter.
   1st KOSB Regt will detail 10 men as carriers for 2 Lt Farrant & 6 men as carriers for 2nd Lt Lewin.
   The officers concerned will arrange direct with the Battalions as to taking over these men & are responsible for arranging that rations are drawn from the Battalions for the carriers.

6) The Mobile Section Section will move out with the attacking Infantry & come into action in positions previously selected as far as possible in front of GREASE TRENCH.
   The mobile Section will move about as circumstances demand & will be prepared to engage at any time any targets which may appear in particular be prepared to engage & if possible silence any hostile machine guns which may open fire.

7.) Men will wear skeleton marching order, box respirators, 3 Sandbags per man & the following extra equipment

  N.C.O.   2 Belt Boxes
  Nº   1   Oil can, Heavy Tripod
  Nº   2   Gun & Light Tripod, Oil Can
  "   3   2 Belt-Boxes, Condenser
  "   4   Spare Parts Box & Shovel
      5   Tin of Water 2 galls & Shovel
      6   2 Belt boxes & Rangefinder
      7   2 Belt-Boxes
      8   2 Belt-Boxes
      9   2 Belt-Boxes.

Nº 8) Officers are responsible that all men are in possession of Iron Rations & a full water bottle. If either Iron Rations or water are used they must be replaced at once. This is of the greatest importance prior to attack. Bully Beef can always be collected from the Rations

9) All officers & N.C.O's will carry a note book & compass

10) Aeroplane contact patrols will be up & flares will be lit in our forward position whenever a contact machine passes overhead "Callying by means of its Klaxon Horn or Very Light."

11) Artillery boards will at once be moved forward to behind the paradas of our forward position.

12) Brigade Head Quarters will not move

13) Company Head Quarters will not move

14) Prisoners will be sent back under armed escort to advanced Cage in LONGUEVAL.
   If handed over to Infantry a receipt should be taken

15) Please acknowledge.

Oct: 23rd 1916

J M Moberly
Lieut & Adjt
87th Machine Gun Coy

Secret.   87th Machine Gun Company Operation Order No 11   Copy No 3
APPENDIX III

1) The XVth & IInd Corps in conjunction with the Reserve Army will attack on the 1st November 1916 at an hour "Zero" to be notified later.
   The 24th Infantry Brigade (on our right) will not be attacking but will assist by bombing up STORMY TRENCH from about N 21 d 5 8 towards our right flank & by Machine Gun & Trench Mortar fire Northwards up the road at N 21 b 6 0.
   The 86th Infty Bde (on our left) will be attacking the lines :— 1st Objective BAYONET TRENCH from about N.20.d.4½.6 to N.20.a.2 9 – 2nd Objective from N.15.c.2.1½ to N.14.c.3 7.

2) The 87th Infty Bde will attack the following lines – 1st Objective from N.21 d 4½.8 to N.21.a.7 8 to N 21 a 0 3 (STORMY TRENCH and trench running S.W. from North end of STORMY TRENCH) 2nd Objective :— from N 21 d 6.5 to N 21 a 7 8 to N 15 c 2 1½. The attack will be carried out by 1st K.O.S.B. on the right & 1st Border Regt on the left.

3) The Brigade boundary on the East will be from our present Right flank to N.21.b.6.0. to N 21.b. 8½. 0. thence Northward.
   The Brigade boundary on the West will be from N.20.d.4.5. to N 15 c 2 2 thence in a North Easterly direction through N.15 c. 4½. 9½.
   The boundary between the 2 Bns in the attacking line will be from N 21 c 4½ 9½ through N 15 d 3 8.
   The bombing post in HILT TRENCH at N 20 d.4½.6. will be handed over to 86th Infty Bde at 1 am on the 1st Nov. 1916
   The communication trench from the Gun Pits to HILT TRENCH & HILT TRENCH from N 20 d 7 4 to N 20 d 6 6 will also be handed over to 86th Infty Bde. at 1 am on the 1st Nov.

4) Action   The assault will be carried out under a creeping Artillery Barrage as follows :—
   a) At Zero the Artillery Barrage will commence on the 1st Objective & the Infantry will at once leave their trenches & get as close to it as possible.
   b) At 0.3. on the Right and 0 4 on the left the creeping barrage will move forward at the rate of 50 yards per minute.
   The 1st objective gained will be consolidated & strong points made at N.21.b.6 0, N.21.b.0 4, N.21.a 7 8. and N 21 a 2 4½
   Companies will advance on a general bearing of 10° True North (23° Magnetic) Each Bn will have a bombing squad on their inner flank to make good any gaps that may occur.
   At 0.10 the personnel for the 2nd Objective will leave the 1st Objective

2.

and will get close to the barrage which will commence to creep at 0.13 at the rate of 50 yards per minute, until it reaches a point 150 yards beyond the 2nd Objective where it will halt.

The personnel to go forward from the 1st Objective are as follows:-

From 1/K.O.S.B:- 2 parties each of ½ Company with 2 Lewis guns to go to N.21.b.6.5. and N.21.b.2.7.

From 1/Border Regt:- one party of ½ Company with 2 Lewis guns to go to the site of a Strong point at N.15.c.3.1.

These parties will make Strong points & throw out patrols to their front to cover the consolidation. These Strong points will be connected up as soon as possible.

Each of these parties will be joined by another ½ Company from the 1st Objective at dusk.

Two bombing squads & 1 platoon will be detailed from 1st Border Regt as mopping up party for the dug-outs in SUNKEN ROAD running from N.20.b.9.3. to N.20.b.6.0.

2/Lt Farrant with 2 guns of No 2 Section will be attached to & will advance with 1/K.O.S.B.Regt:- As soon as the first objective is gained one of these guns will be placed in the strong point being built at N.21.b.6.0. & the other in the Strong point being built at N.21.b.0.4.

2/Lt Downes with 2 guns of No 4 Section will be attached to & will advance with 1st/Border Regt:- As soon as the 1st Objective is gained one of these guns will be placed in the Strong point being built at N.21.a.7.8. & the other in the Strong point being built at N.21.a.2.4½.

2/Lt Lewin with 2 guns of No 2 Section will act as a roving detachment on the right flank, & 2/Lt Hunter with 2 guns of No 4 Section will act as a roving detachment on the left flank.

These guns will follow up the barrage and will deal with any opposition on the flanks, & will rejoin the attacking troops after the objective has been gained.

On reaching the new line 2/Lt Lewin will place one gun in the Strong point at N.21.b.6.0 & will hold the other gun in reserve to replace casualties — 2/Lt Hunter will place one gun in the strong point at N.21.a.7.8 and the other in the Strong point at N.21.a.2.4½.

2 guns of No 3 Section under 2/Lt Payne will fire on BAYONET TRENCH from zero to 05 from positions in the communication trench at N.20.d.5.4 to cover the advance. At 05 these guns will lift on to BARLEY TRENCH.

3

The remaining 2 guns of Nº 3 Section & 4 guns of Nº 1 Sections will be under 2/Lt Green & will cover the advance by firing on BACON TRENCH & BARLEY TRENCH respectively from positions at approximately N 26 a 4.0. The 2 guns of Nº 3 Section at N 26 a 40 will fire on BACON TRENCH from 0.0 to 0.6 when they will lift on to BARLEY TRENCH

5) 10 men from 1st Border Regt will be attached to 2/Lt Downes & 6 men to 2/Lt Hunter as a carrying party & 10 men from 1st KOSB will be attached to 2/Lt Farrant & 6 men to 2/Lt Lewin. These parties will be at Bde HQ at 12 noon on the 31st inst. They will be met & guided up to Nº 4 Section & Nº 2 Section respectively by guides from Coy H.Q.

6) Rations
2nd/Lt Green will be responsible for getting rations up to Nºs 2 & 4 Sections on the evening of the 1st Nov. 8 men will report to him from Coy H.Q. on the morning of 1st Nov for this purpose & for the replacing of casualties

7) Officers of Nº 2 & 4 Section will send back messages to 2/Lt Green in GIRD TRENCH as soon as possible after reaching objective, giving the situation & stating how many men are required to replace casualties etc:-

8) One Officer & 30 men of the Royal Engineers will assist in the construction of the strong points in the 1st Objective. They will return to camp at daylight.

9) Two companies of the Pioneers will each dig a communication trench forward from GREASE TRENCH, one from N 21 c 6 9 to strong point at N 21 b 0 4 the other from N 21 c 2 9 to strong point at N 21 a 2 4½.

10) Equipment will be carried as already detailed

11) A forward dump is established at N 26 a 9 9 from which S.A.A. Sandbags etc:- can be drawn. A reserve of 100 tins of water & 400 Iron Rations will be stored at this dump

12) 2 Contact Aeroplanes will be in the air from 0.3 for 2 hours after which one contact aeroplane will be up until dark. Troops will indicate their positions to them by means of a group of 6 red flares. Flares will be lit:-
    a) on reaching 1st Objective
    b) on reaching 2nd Objective
    c) at certain stated times to be ordered later

13) The Officers commanding 1st KOSB & 1st Border Regts will be in dug outs at Gun Pits from which telephone lines have been

laid to their old Bn H.Q. — Runners from the front line will deliver their messages at the Gun Pits.

14) Unwounded prisoners will be sent down under escort to the Corps Cage at S.28.a.2.2. (South of LONGUEVAL) when they will be handed over & the escort will rejoin their units. Escorts will call at Bde H.Q. on their way to the Cage.

15) Stretcher bearer relay posts are established at N.26.c.6.1 & collecting posts with a medical Officer at each) at N.31.b.4.0 and N.32.c.0.8.

A main collecting post under a medical Officer is established at S.6.b.8.0 (South FLERS) when lying down cases will be evacuated by Decauville Railway to LONGUEVAL.

16) Watches will be synchronised from nearest Bn H Q at 10 am and 8 PM on the 31st inst. & at 10 a m on the 1st Nov.

17) Please acknowledge.

Issued at . . . . .

Copy No 1 — Office
" 2 & 3 — War Diary
" 4 — 2/Lt Hunter
" 5 — 2/Lt Downes
" 6 — 2/Lt Payne
" 7 — 2/Lt Farrant
" 8 — 2/Lt Lavin
" 9 — 2/Lt Green
" 10 — 87th Infy Bde
" 11 — 1st Border Regt
" 12 — 1st KOSB Regt
" 13 — 86th M G Coy
" 14 — 88th M G Coy

J H Moberly.
Lieut & Adjt
87th Machine Gun Coy

29th Division.
87th Infantry Brigade.

87th MACHINE GUN COMPANY

NOVEMBER 1 9 1 6

CONFIDENTIAL.

WAR DIARY

of

87th Machine Gun Company.

From 1st November 1916 to 30th November 1916.

(VOLUME 6.)

WAR DIARY
or
INTELLIGENCE SUMMARY
(Erase heading not required.)

Army Form C.

Instructions regarding War Diaries and Intelligence Summaries are contained in F.S. Regs., Part II. and the Staff Manual respectively. Title Pages will be prepared in manuscript.

Place	Date	Hour	Summary of Events and Information	Remarks and references to Appendices
FRICOURT	1st		1 O.R. taken on strength of Company.	
	2nd		8 O.R. taken on strength of Company.	
	3rd		Coy marched to ALBERT station & proceeded by train from there to AIRAINES, where they went into Billets. Transport did not accompany units but proceeded to CORBIE.	
AIRAINES	7th		2 O.R. evacuated to C.C.S.	
"	11th		1 O.R. evacuated to C.C.S.	
"	12th		1 O.R. evacuated to C.C.S.	
CITADEL	14th 9p.m.		Coy left AIRAINES & proceeded by motor bus to BOIRE, from where they marched to CITADEL CAMP, near FRICOURT, arriving about 6 p.m. Transport rejoined Coy.	
BRICQUETERIE	15th 9 p.m.		Coy marched to BRICQUETERIE Camp where they remained for night.	
GUILLEMONT	16th		Coy relieved 25th M.G. Coy in the line near LES BOEUFS. No. 2 Section (ten 1 gun) proceeded to front line (BENNETT TRENCH) No. 4 Section proceeded to 2nd line (ANTELOPE TRENCH)	

Army Form C. 2118.

WAR DIARY
or
INTELLIGENCE SUMMARY
(Erase heading not required.)

Instructions regarding War Diaries and Intelligence Summaries are contained in F. S. Regs., Part II. and the Staff Manual respectively. Title Pages will be prepared in manuscript.

Place	Date	Hour	Summary of Events and Information	Remarks and references to Appendices
GUILLEMONT	16th (contd)		No. 3 section proceeded to 3rd line (Ox TRENCH) Coy H.Q., near GUILLEMONT.	
"	18th		No. 1 section in reserve at Coy H.Q. 6 O.R. taken on strength of Company. Section relief completed as follows:— No. 4 section proceeded to BENNETT TRENCH No. 3 " " " ANTELOPE ———— No. 1 " " " OX ———— No. 2 " " " Coy H.Q.	
	20th		Section relief completed on the same principle as above, such section moving forward one line. 1 O.R. (attached) killed in Action. 2 O.R. Killed in Action.	
	21st			
	22nd		Section relief completed on the same principle as above.	
	19th		2 guns were placed in position against hostile aircraft, one in OX TRENCH and one just E. of the FLERS LINE.	
	23rd		1 O.R. evacuated to C.C.S.	

Army Form C. 2118.

WAR DIARY
or
INTELLIGENCE SUMMARY

(Erase heading not required.)

Place	Date	Hour	Summary of Events and Information	Remarks and references to Appendices
GUILLEMONT	24th		Coy relieved from the line by 66th M.G. Coy. Nos 3 & 4 sections marched down to CARNOY CAMP. Nos 1 & 2 sections remaining for the night at Coy H.Q. near GUILLEMONT.	
CARNOY	25th		Nos 1 & 2 sections rejoined the remainder of Coy at CARNOY. 1 O.R. struck off strength of Company.	

J.R. Bruill
Major
Comdg 89 Machine Gun Coy.

29th Division.

87th Infantry Brigade

87th MACHINE GUN COMPANY

DECEMBER 1 9 1 6

CONFIDENTIAL.

WAR DIARY

of

87th Machine Gun Company.

From 1st December 1916 to 31st December 1916.

(Volume 7.)

WAR DIARY
or
INTELLIGENCE SUMMARY

Army Form C. 2118.

Place	Date	Hour	Summary of Events and Information	Remarks and references to Appendices
CARNOY	1st	—	4 O.R. evacuated sick out of Divl Area. 1 O.R. evacuated to No 44 Prisoners of War Cage (under age)	
"	3rd		Coy relieved 86th M.G. Coy in the trenches in front of LESBOEUFS (Left sector) No. 3 Section proceeded to front line - 2 " " " Second line (TOW TRENCH) - 4 " " " Third line (FLERS LINE) - 1 " remained in reserve at Coy H.Q.	
LESBOEUFS	5th		1 O.R. killed & 2 O.R. wounded by shell fire during relief	
	7th		3 O.R. killed & 1 wounded by shell fire. Section relief as follows:— No. 4 Section relieved No. 3 Section	
	8th		Approval obtained from 6/7th Infy Bde for R.E. to start work on improving deep dug-outs in THISTLE TRENCH, with a view to placing 3 Machine Guns there M. gun in SUMMER TRENCH (N.35.c.2.9.) moved to ZENITH TRENCH (N.34.b.9.5.), thus covering front line from ZENITH TRENCH to North end of FALL TRENCH.	
	9th		Present co-ordinates & areas of fire of the 72 guns in the line are as follows:— (Ref:- Map Sheet 57c S.W.)	

WAR DIARY or INTELLIGENCE SUMMARY

Army Form C. 2118.

(Erase heading not required.)

Place	Date	Hour	Summary of Events and Information	Remarks and references to Appendices
LESBOEUFS	9th		N35c.7.2. ..... 35° to 100°. T3a.7.3 ..... Zero to 95°. N35c.7½.4 ..... 10° to 90°. T3d.3.3 ..... 30° to 90°. N34.8½.4 ..... 70° to 135°. T9d.4.9 ..... 20° to 80°. N34.7.2. ..... 135° to 185°. T8d.9.8 ..... Zero to 60°. N34c.4.7 ..... 70° to 140° (1 C. Gun) T8d.8.1 ..... 90° to 140°. ..... 10° to 80° (4th Gun) (2 guns) (2 guns) Casualties. 5 O.R. evacuated (sick) out of Div. Area. 1 O.R. wounded by shell fire. Gun position in OZONE AVENUE hit by a shell, + gun damaged. Coy relieved from the line by 60th M.G. Coy. Relief started at 11am., complete at 7.30 p.m.	
	11th		Coy marched to CITADEL CAMP.	
CITADEL	12th		Coy marched to MERICOURT, where they were billeted for the night.	
MERICOURT	13th		Coy marched to EDGE HILL and entrained for HANGEST, where they arrived at 7 p.m. From there they marched to Billets at SOUES (Transport marched by road from MERICOURT to SOUES). 4 O.R. taken on strength from Base Depot.	

Army Form C. 2118.

WAR DIARY
or
INTELLIGENCE SUMMARY
(Erase heading not required.)

Instructions regarding War Diaries and Intelligence Summaries are contained in F. S. Regs., Part II. and the Staff Manual respectively. Title Pages will be prepared in manuscript.

Place	Date	Hour	Summary of Events and Information	Remarks and references to Appendices
SOUES	18th		2 O.R. evacuated (sick) out of Divisional Area.	
"	19th		1 O.R. " " " "	
"	20th		Coy inspected in marching order (with Transport) by G.O.C. 87th Inf Bde.	
"	21st		1 O.R. struck off strength of Coy on being transferred to 62 M.G. Coy.	
"	26th		1 O.R. taken on strength of Coy.	
"	27th		2 O.R. evacuated (sick) out of Div. Area.	
"	28th		Coy inspected in marching order (with Transport) by G.O.C. 87th Inf Bde.	
"	30th		1 O.R. evacuated (sick) out of Div. Area.	

H.R. Bennill
Major
Commdg 87th Machine Gun Coy.

Vol 8.

CONFIDENTIAL.

WAR DIARY

OF

87th Machine Gun Company.

FROM January 1st 1917 TO January 31st 1917.

VOLUME 8

WAR DIARY
or
INTELLIGENCE SUMMARY

(Erase heading not required.)

Army Form C. 2118.

Instructions regarding War Diaries and Intelligence Summaries are contained in F.S. Regs., Part II. and the Staff Manual respectively. Title Pages will be prepared in manuscript.

Place	Date	Hour	Summary of Events and Information	Remarks and references to Appendices
In the Field	1.7.19		Machine Gun Operation Order No. 15 issued.	
	2.7.19		Draft from CAMIERS of 1 Lance Corporal 28 O.R.	
	3.7.19		5 O.R. Evacuated Sick out of Divisional Area.	
	6.7.19		1 O.R. Transferred from 1st Royal Inniskilling Fusiliers and taken on strength of Company.	
			1 O.R. Evacuated sick out of Divisional Area.	
	7.7.19		Company Inoculated TAB. Pte CUMMINGS sent to Divisional Rest Company.	
	11.7.19		3 O.R. Evacuated out of Divl. Area. At 1400 transport left SOUES for BRESLE.	
			Under Brigade transport officer.	
	12.7.19		Company marched from SOUES to HANGEST STATION Entrained for MERICOURT.	
	13.7.19		Marched from MERICOURT to BRESLE arriving about 1330.	
			2 O.R. Evacuated out of Divisional Area. 1 O.R. Attached from 1st Royal Inniskilling Fusiliers and taken on strength of Company.	
	14.7.19		Company and transport marched from BRESLE at 0930 to MANSEL CAMP arriving about 1500.	
	15.7.19		Company marched from MANSEL CAMP to GUILLEMONT STATION (Company H.Q.) and entrained 51st M.G. Coy. one other unit.	
			No. 2 Section proceeded to York Loop.	
			No. 3 " " " "	
			No. 4 " " to Sabbat Line.	
			No. 1 " " to FLERS LINE	
			" " " Received in Reinforcements 4 O.R. to Company H.Q.	
	18.7.19		1 O.R. Taken on strength of Company from Base.	
	19.7.19		No. 1 Section relieved No. 2 "	
			No. 4 " " " No. 3 "	
	20.7.19		1 O.R. Evacuated sick out of Divisional Area.	

WAR DIARY or INTELLIGENCE SUMMARY

Army Form C. 2118.

(Erase heading not required.)

Instructions regarding War Diaries and Intelligence Summaries are contained in F. S. Regs., Part II. and the Staff Manual respectively. Title Pages will be prepared in manuscript.

Place	Date	Hour	Summary of Events and Information	Remarks and references to Appendices
In the field	22.1.17 23.1.17		1 O.R. taken on strength of Company from 141st Heavy Machine Gun Section Bedford. No. 3 Section to front line No. 2 " " " No. 1 " FLERS LINE No. 4 " Coy. H.Q.	
	24.1.17		1 O.R. evacuated sick out of Dunlouse Camp. J.O.R. hurnt attd on account of Gonsdn of Transfer. Syn N.W. Operation Order	
	25.1.17		No. 14 issued. 88 M.G. Coy. took over 2 positions from this Company. No. 4 Section to front Line No. 3 " " " No. 2 " Second Line No. 1 " FLERS LINE	
	26.1.17		No. 2 & 1 Section to front Line No. 4 " Second Line No. 3 " FLERS LINE. Casualties 4 O.R. killed by shell fire. 2 O.R. missing 16 O.R. wounded by shell fire.	
	29.1.17		Report on Machine Gun Operations carried out by my Coy in most attacks Nos 1 & 4 Sections to front Line No. 3 " " FLERS LINE No. 2 " Second Line	
	30.1.17		1 O.R. evacuated sick to Divisional Baths	

WAR DIARY
or
INTELLIGENCE SUMMARY

Army Form C. 2118.

Place	Date	Hour	Summary of Events and Information	Remarks and references to Appendices
In the Field	31-1-17		1 O.R. evacuated out of divisional area. Company relieved by 585 M.G. Coy at dusk. Company proceeded to BRIQUETERIE CAMP. Transport remaining at CARNOY.	

J.R. Bennett
Major
Comdg 81st M.S. Coy.

SECRET   87th Machine Gun Company.   Copy No 2
                      Operation Order No 14

Reference. Trench Map.   In the Field
Scale 1/10,000   25/1/17.

1. **OBJECTIVE.**   The 87th Infantry Brigade Group will attack the enemy's line from N.36.d.4.2. to N.35.d.8.0. early on the 27th January 1917.

       1st Objective, marked BLUE on attached diagram.
       2nd Objective, marked RED on attached diagram.

Strong points will be made as follows.

(a) 1. About ERSATZ POINT
     2. About N.36.d.3.4.
     3. Intermediate posts as ground admits

(b) 1. About the ROAD JUNCTION. N.36.c.7.1.
     2. About N.35.d.8.1.
     3. Intermediate Posts as ground admits.

Boundaries of the attack and limits of the Objective are as follows.

    RIGHT.   A line drawn from N.36.d.4½.0. through N.36.b.1.6.
    LEFT.   A line drawn from T.5.b.9.3. through N.35.b.9.0.

The Brigades on either side will assist with Machine Gun fire and a mobile Section of the 88th Brigade will operate with and protect the right flank of the attack.

2. **ACTION.**   No 4 Section will act as a MOBILE Section to protect the left flank and centre of the attack and will form up by 0200 on the 27th inst.   In or in front of LINCOLN TRENCH at T.6.a.6.8. they will advance to the first Objective with and immediately behind the SECOND wave of the assaulting troops. As soon as the THIRD wave has passed on to the Second Objective No 4 Section will advance beyond the first Objective and Take up positions near the GUN PITS at N.36.c.6.2. to Cover the LEFT flank and FRONT of the new line, particularly LANDWEHR TRENCH, HAIL TRENCH, SUNKEN ROAD in N.36.a. and MOON TRENCH.

No 3. Section will occupy positions in FALL & BENNETT TRENCHES, and will cover the LEFT flank of the attack & Objective when gained.

LEFT 2 GUNS will fire on N.36.a.6.0. using 50 yards differences.
RIGHT 2 GUNS will fire on HAIL TRENCH.

No. 2 Section (less 2 guns) and 2 Guns of No. 1 Section will occupy positions in ANTELOPE TRENCH and will cover the LEFT flank of the attack.

LEFT 2 GUNS will traverse LANDWEHR TRENCH from N.35.d.3.5. to N.35.d.5½.2½.

RIGHT 2 GUNS will traverse LANDWEHR TRENCH from N.35.d.0.7. to N.35.d.3.5.

Right Guns will occasionally elevate and search up the valley to N.35.b.1.0.

No. 1 SECTION (less 2 Guns) & 2 Guns of No. 2 Section will occupy the ordinary defensive positions in COW TRENCH, OX TRENCH (2) and near TANK. They will be prepared to move forward if required.

Flash blinders will be used and in addition all guns will be screened with sandbags to hide the frontal flash.

3. RATE OF FIRE.
From 00 to 0.25 all guns will open rapid fire on targets as detailed in para: 2.
From 0.25 to 0.45 all guns will fire a long burst every five minutes.
At 0.45 Guns except those of No. 3 Section will cease fire but will open fire in case of S.O.S. Signal, HOSTILE counter attack or any target being presented.
No. 3 Section will continue to fire a long burst every 5 minutes till 2.00

4. REGISTRATION. will be carried out at intervals on the days preceding the attack, care being taken to avoid arousing the suspicion of the enemy

5. NON FREEZING MIXTURE
During the frost, only 5 pints will be put in the Barrel Casing and 20% of glycerine mixed with the water. Guns will be oiled sparingly until warm.

6. RANGE CARDS
Previous to the operation range cards will be made on the assumption that the position has been taken.

7. CARRIERS
A carrying party of 2 N.C.O's and 20 men from the 1st K.O.S.B. will report at ANTELOPE TRENCH at 2300 on the 26th inst. This party will be attached to No. 4 Section and will be sent

back when the objective is reached & the guns are in position. In any case not later than dawn.

8. ARTILLERY.

At ZERO an artillery barrage will be placed on the German line. The Infantry will at once leave their trenches and advance as close to the barrage as possible. A smoke barrage will be placed on STAR & MOOR TRENCHES and smoke candles will be let off from FALL TRENCH if the wind is favourable.

9. ZERO HOUR

The opening of the artillery barrage is the signal for Zero. A time will be stated as a guide only.

10. S.O.S.

The S.O.S. Signal is either 3 Rockets in the following order. GREEN – WHITE – GREEN, or a special pattern Rifle Grenade Rocket bursting into 2 RED & 2 GREEN Stars. Either Signal will have the desired effect.

11. CONTACT AEROPLANE.

A contact Aeroplane will be in the air about an hour after dawn and flares will be lighted by troops in the most forward position when called for by the Aeroplane.

12. RESERVE DUMPS.

Reserve Dumps of S.A.A, Bombs, Very lights, S.O.S. Rockets, Rations and Water, have been made at T.6.a.20.15. and T.6.b.25.50. A R.E. Dump for wire screw picquets, Sandbags etc:- has been formed at T.6.a.3.7.

13. PAPERS.

Troops taking part in the attack will not carry any maps or papers containing information of value to the enemy.

14. WATCHES.

Sections will send an orderly to synchronize watches at Advance Company Headquarters (ANTELOPE) at 2300 on 26th inst.

15. COMMUNICATION TRENCH.

A Communication Trench will be dug from T.6.a 6.7. to T.6.a 6.9.

16. HEADQUARTERS.

Advanced Company Headquarters will be established at 1800 on the 26th inst. in the deep dug out in ANTELOPE TRENCH all reports will be sent there.

17. REPORTS.
Section Officers will send in a report giving general situation, Casualties & Rounds fired, by 20 00 on the 27th inst:. In addition O/C. N° 4 Section will send back report as above by carrying party on the morning of the 27th inst:

18. AID POSTS.
Aid posts will be established in deep dug outs at T.10.a.8.6. and T.10.c.8.4.

19. Please ACKNOWLEDGE

H C Randall
Lieut & Adjt
87th Machine Gun Company.

Issued at 1400

Copy 1-3. Office
    4 — 87th Infantry Brigade
    5 — 2nd South Wales Bd
    6 — 1st Kings Own Scottish Bds
    7 — 1st Royal Inniskilling Fusrs
    8 — 1st Border Regt
    9 — 86th Machine Gun Company
    10 — 88th Machine Gun Company
    11 — 8th Australian Machine Gun Company.
12-17 — Section Officers

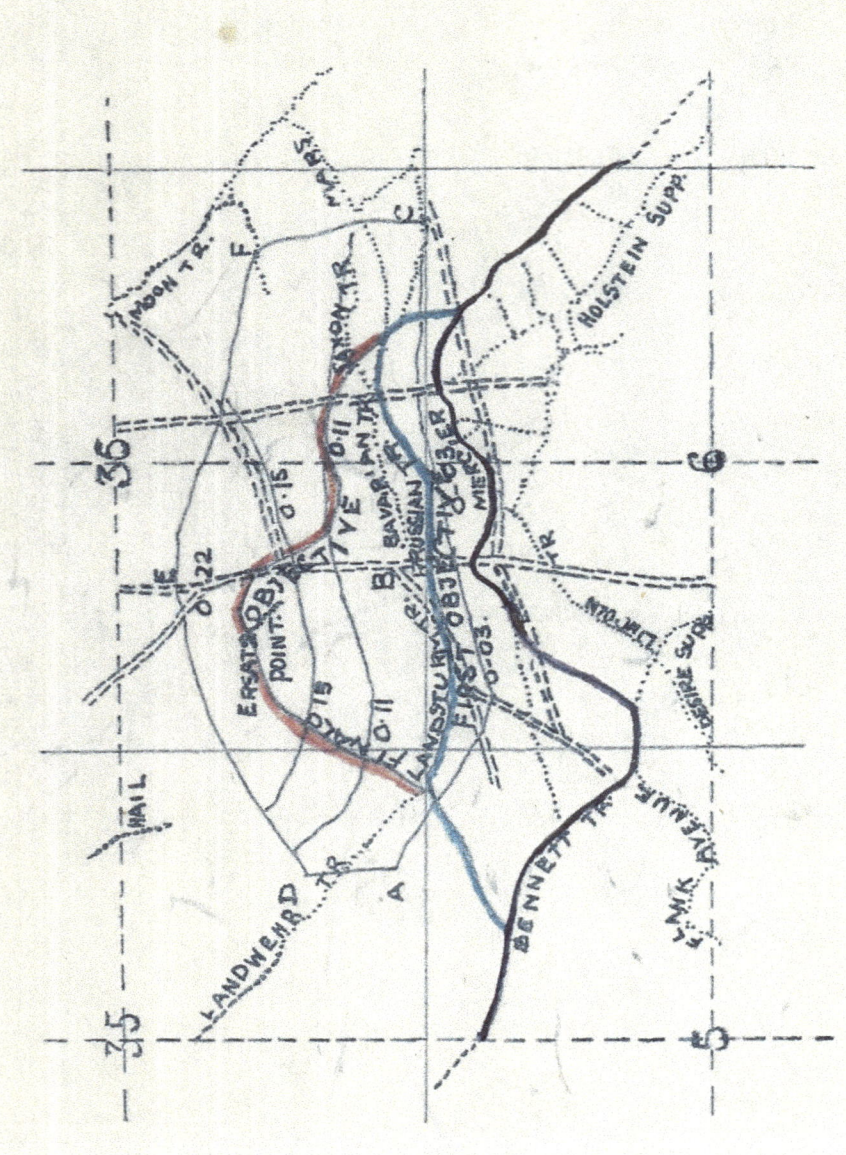

Report on Machine Gun Operations on the 27th inst.-

<u>1</u> Disposition of Machine Guns for the attack - See Company Operation Order No 14   Copy attached

<u>2</u>. The Mobile Section under 2/LT G.S.J. DOWNES got into position at 0030 on the 27th inst & were fully informed by 2/LT DOWNES about their duties and the general direction of the attack. The Section and carrying party attached were arranged in column of Gun teams at 5 to 10 yards distance the men being extended to 2 paces interval & all Gun equipment & stores were placed out in no mansland previously to obviate delay in climbing out of the trench. The Section except for a sentry returned to the trench until 10 minutes before Zero at which time they went out & formed up in no mansland on their loads, which were already there. At Zero the Section led by 2/LT G.S.J. DOWNES advanced with the Second Wave of the Infantry and came into action 100 yards beyond the first objective. They at once proceeded to dig in 2 Guns covering MOON TRENCH. One Gun CEMETERY CIRCLE & One Gun HAIL TRENCH. No targets were seen during the advance except unarmed parties advancing to Surrender.

One Gun with its team were destroyed by one of our Shrapnel Shells, falling short at 20 minutes after Zero. At 40 minutes after Zero after consultation with Infantry Commanders the Guns were retired to the captured German trench owing to the difficulty of digging in. Machine Gun positions were made & alternative positions noted.

<u>Casualties</u> - Only one casualty occured during the advance but the Section suffered severely from Shell fire losing

    Killed 1 O.R.
    Wounded - 2/LT G.S.J. DOWNES
      "   5. O.R.
    Missing - 3. O.R.

The carrying party also sustained casualties. The Section were relieved by half Sections by 2300 on the 27th inst &

proceeded to the Support Line.

No 3 Section in FALL TRENCH & BENNETT TR. was relieved by No 1 Section in the early morning of the 28th after the first relief had been completed proceeded to the Intermediate Line (FLERS LINE)

Points noticed — The attack was so successful that the advantages of a mobile Section were not fully illustrated. The advantage of not being under the orders of an Infantry Company Commander were greatly appreciated by the officer commanding the mobile Section, who was enabled to place his Guns to the best tactical advantage with a full knowledge of all supporting machine Guns in rear.

In the Field
29/1/17.

J.H.R. Bennell
Major
Commd. 87th Machine Gun Coy

CONFIDENTIAL

War Diary

of

87th Machine Gun Company.

From 1st February.1917. to 28th February.1917

(VOLUME 9)

Army Form C. 2118.

WAR DIARY
or
INTELLIGENCE SUMMARY
(Erase heading not required.)

Instructions regarding War Diaries and Intelligence Summaries are contained in F.S. Regs., Part II. and the Staff Manual respectively. Title Pages will be prepared in manuscript.

Place	Date	Hour	Summary of Events and Information	Remarks and references to Appendices
In the Field	July 1917 5/6/17		One Section picked from Company proceeded to LANDWEHR TRENCH	
	5/6		Company, less one Section, relieved by 60th Machine Gun Company marched from BRIQUETERIE to MEAULTE, with Transport.	
	6th			
	7th		No.3 Section proceeded to FLESSELES for anti-aircraft duty.	
	8th		One Section relieved from front line & returned to MEAULTE	
			Draft of 30 other ranks arrived from CAMIERS.	
	12th		2/Lieut O.S.J. DOWNES awarded Military Cross.	
	15th		No.1 Section relieved No.3 Section at FLESSELES on anti-aircraft duty.	
	20th		Company marched to BRONFAY, Camp No.108. Transports at No.15. Camp.	
	21st		No.1 Section returned from FLESSELES.	
	23rd		7 Other Ranks evacuated sick out of Divisional Area.	
	24th		Lieut S.G. OUTHIN taken on strength of Company from Base.	
	25th		Operation Order No.15 issued (See App.)	See App. I
	26th		12 Guns (Nos 2, 3, & 4 Sections) proceeded to the line & took up indirect fire positions in BULL DOG RESERVE. These guns were attached to O.C. 88th M.G. Company.	
			2 Guns of No.1 Section proceeded to the line & took up positions on the Intermediate Line (for defensive purposes). These guns were attached to O.C. 86th M.G. Company.	
	27th		2 O.R. Struck off Strength of Company on proceeding for duty to U.K. - 7 Other ranks taken on strength of Company from Base.	

2449 Wt. W14957/M90 750,000 1/16 J.B.C. & A. Forms/C.2118/12.

Army Form C. 2118.

WAR DIARY
or
INTELLIGENCE SUMMARY

(Erase heading not required.)

Place	Date	Hour	Summary of Events and Information	Remarks and references to Appendices
In the Field	Feb 28th		Attack on German Trenches East of SAILLY-SAILLISEL by 86th Infantry Brigade. The 12 Guns of 87th Machine Gun Company attached to 88th Machine Gun Company supported the attack with Indirect Overhead Fire on the SUNKEN ROAD. Fire was opened at Zero & maintained for One & a half hours. Expenditure of S.A.A. 26,000 rounds.	

G Mulvey
Lieut.
Comm'd 87; Machine Gun Company

87th Machine Gun Company   Copy No. 2

Operation Order No. 15.

SECRET.

In the Field
25th Feb. 1917.

1. **Objective**

The 86th Brigade will attack the German Trenches East of SAILLY-SAILLISEL from U14b 85.25 to U8d 45.90. The 87th Machine Gun Company will support the attack with indirect overhead fire.

2. **Reports & Communications**

All reports & communications will be sent to O.C. 88th Machine Gun Company.

3. **Disposition of Machine Guns.**

Nos. 2, 3, & 4 Sections (12 guns) under Lt. A.W. Tarrant & Lt. S.G. Outwin will occupy positions in BULL DOG RESERVE. These guns will fire on the SUNKEN ROAD from U9c 2.7. to U9a 3.9. All guns will be screened by sandbags to hide the frontal flash. Two guns of No. 1 Section will be placed at T18a 6.7. & T18a 8.2. for defensive purposes, & will be under the orders of O.C. 86th Machine Gun Company.

4. **Opening of Fire.**

Full barrage fire will be opened at Zero and maintained for 1½ hours.

5. **Registration.**

Registration will not take place. The Guns consequently will be laid with the greatest precision.

6. **Ammunition.**

In addition to the full complement of belt boxes, 30,000 rounds S.A.A. will be drawn from the dump on the FREGICOURT ROAD.

7. **Water Supply.**

One petrol tin of water will be placed at each gun position. This water will be treated with 25% of Glycerine.

8. **Zero Hour.**

This will be the moment at which the artillery barrage falls.

9. **Certificate.**

Lieut. A.W. Tarrant will render a certificate to O.C. 88th Machine Gun Company by 6 p.m. on the 27th inst., stating (1) That all guns are in position & ready to open fire. (2) That 30,000 rounds reserve S.A.A. have been placed at the gun positions. (3) That each gun has a supply of water treated with non-freezing mixture. (4) The exact targets to be engaged by the 12 guns. (5) That all gun numbers understand thoroughly what is required of them.

10. **Oil & Spare Parts.**

A reserve of oil & a complete set of spare parts will be maintained at each gun.

H.C. Randall

Lieut. & adjt.
87th Machine Gun Company

Copies.
- No. 1 — Office
- 2 & 3 — War Diary
- 4 — Lt. A.W. Tarrant
- 5 — Lt. R.C. Green
- 6 — Lt. S.G. Ortwin
- 7 — 87th Inf. Bde
- 8 — 86th M.G. Coy
- 9 — 88th M.G. Coy

Vol 10

CONFIDENTIAL.

WAR DIARY
of
87th Machine Gun Company.

From 1st March 1917 to 31st March 1917.

(VOLUME 10)

Army Form C. 2118.

WAR DIARY
INTELLIGENCE SUMMARY

(Erase heading not required.)

Instructions regarding War Diaries and Intelligence Summaries are contained in F. S. Regs., Part II. and the Staff Manual respectively. Title Pages will be prepared in manuscript.

Place	Date	Hour	Summary of Events and Information	Remarks and references to Appendices
CORBIE	3rd		1 O.R. wounded by Shell fire. No. 2, 3, 4, & 5 No. 1 Section relieved from the trenches.	
BRONFAY	4th		Company entrained at PLATEAU at 4 p.m., detraining at CORBIE, from where they marched to Billets at BUSSY. Transport proceeds at 8 p.m. by road to BUSSY, arriving at 3 p.m.	
BUSSY	5th		1 O.R. sent to United Kingdom as Machine Gun Instructor.	
"	8th		Inspection of Company by G.O.C. 87th Inf. Brigade. 1 O.R. sent to United Kingdom for munition work. 4 O.R. evacuated (sick) out of Divisional Area.	
"	10th		2 O.R. taken on strength of Company. 2 O.R. evacuated (sick) out of Divisional Area.	
"	15th		Major H.R. BORRILL returned from M.G.C. Base, resumed command of Company.	
"	18th		Company transport left BUSSY by road for SOUES, being billeted for the night at ARGOEUVES.	

WAR DIARY or **INTELLIGENCE SUMMARY**

(Erase heading not required.)

Army Form C. 2118.

Place	Date	Hour	Summary of Events and Information	Remarks and references to Appendices
BUSSY	19th		Company marched from BUSSY to EDGEHILL, where they entrained for AIRAINES. Marched from AIRAINES to SOUES, arriving at 12.15 A.m. March 20th.	
SOUES	24th		Lieut W.H. LEWIN struck off strength of Company (evacuated sick to U.K.) 1 O.R. transferred to 1st Machine Gun Company.	
"	25th		3 O.R. evacuated (sick) out of Divisional Area. At 11 p.m. all clocks were advanced one hour.	
"	26th		Company took part in a Divisional Scheme of attack in open warfare.	
"	27th		Company took part in Brigade Scheme of attack in open warfare.	
"	29th		Company marched with transport from SOUES to VIGNACOURT, where they were billeted.	
VIGNACOURT	30th		Company marched from VIGNACOURT to billets in FIEFFES. 4 O.R. evacuated (sick) out of Divisional Area.	

J.W. Murrill
Major
Comm'g 87th Machine Gun Company

CONFIDENTIAL

WAR DIARY

of

87th Machine Gun Company

for

1st April 1917 to 30th April 1917.

(VOLUME II)

WAR DIARY
or
INTELLIGENCE SUMMARY

Army Form C. 2118.

Place	Date	Hour	Summary of Events and Information	Remarks and references to Appendices
FIEFFES	1st		Company marched from FIEFFES to Billets in WEM	
WEM	2nd		Company marched from WEM to huts at LUCHEUX.	
LUCHEUX	3rd		1 O.R. evacuated out of Divl. Area. 1 O.R. rejoined from C.C.S. 6 O.R. taken on strength from Base.	
"	4th		19 O.R. taken on strength of Company from Base.	
"	5th		Company marched (with Transport) to ETREE-WAMIN.	
ETREE-WAMIN	7th		Company marched to WARLUZEL.	
WARLUZEL	8th		Company marched to BAVINCOURT.	
BAVINCOURT	11th		Orders issued for Bde. to be ready to move at 2 hours notice.	
"	12th		Company left BAVINCOURT at 9 a.m. & marched with Transport, as part of Divisional Column, to ARRAS, where they arrived about 4:30 p.m. At 7 p.m. Company started from ARRAS to relieve 35th M.G. Coy in the FEUCHY-CHAPEL sector. Owing to congested state of roads guns were not in position till 5 a.m. following morning. Disposition of guns as follows:— No 1 Section (4 guns) on ORANGE HILL. No 2. (4 guns) in BROWN LINE just South of ARRAS-CAMBRAI road. No 3 & 4 Sections in Reserve at Coy H.Q. (Brown line 500 yds North of ARRAS-CAMBRAI road.)	
FEUCHY	14th		No 2, 3, & 4 Sections moved to GUEMAPPE sector to position Selected for covering attack on GUEMAPPE. 1 O.R. wounded by shell fire.	
GUEMAPPE SECTOR	15th		Attack on GUEMAPPE postponed. 1 O.R. wounded by shell fire. Coy. H.Q. moved to dugout in N10.d. 2 guns of No 4 section moved from N17 & 19 to N11.c.6.2. 1 gun of No 3 section moved from N11.d.1.2. to front line at N12 & 81 to cover front line in front of GUEMAPPE.	
"	16th		Another gun of No 3 Section moved from N11.d.1.2. to front line N12 & 81. No 1 Section positions in vicinity of 88th M.G. Coy in vicinity of LA BERGERE.	(N12.d.8.8)
"	17th		No 1 Section retired & guns of 88th M.G. Coy in vicinity of ORANGE HILL evacuated.	

Army Form C. 2118.

WAR DIARY
or
INTELLIGENCE SUMMARY
(Erase heading not required.)

Instructions regarding War Diaries and Intelligence Summaries are contained in F. S. Regs., Part II. and the Staff Manual respectively. Title Pages will be prepared in manuscript.

Place	Date	Hour	Summary of Events and Information	Remarks and references to Appendices
GUEMAPPS Sector	18th		Information received of expected German relief in this sector during night of 18th/19th. All M.G.'s kept up except those in front line fires intermittently during night on enemy's lines of approach behind his front line.	
"	19th		1 O.R. admitted sick out of Bn. HQrs. Coy relieved from the trenches by 44th, 145th, & 88th M.G. Coys, & proceeded to rest billets in ARRAS. 3 O.R. wounded by shell fire.	see App. I.
ARRAS	21st		Congratulation Order No. 16 (issued) 1 O.R. wounded but remained at duty. 2 Sections proceeded to the line & occupied position in MONCHY-LE-PREUX.	
"	22nd		Remaining 2 Section & HQ moved up to MONCHY-LE-PREUX. 1 O.R. killed in action.	
MONCHY	23rd		Coy took part in a Gen'l attack on German trenches at 4.45 A.M. The Division in question sustained heavy casualties but got 2 guns up to 1st objective & maintained them there. Remaining 6 sections did barrage fire during the day & were fired on both by the 2 forward guns & also by the other sections. These targets included several German Counter attacks which were held up largely by our M.G. fire. 6 O.R. taken as strength. Casualties:- Killed 3 O.R. Wounded: Lt. A.F. LEDWARD & 16 O.R. Missing 1 O.R.	see App. II.
"	24th		Shelling very spasmodic reduced on both sides from that on 23rd inst. A further attack was made at 4 p.m. by 86th Inf. Bde. in which the three rear sections participated with Barrage fire. During the night (which was very calm) the Coy was relieved by 8th M.G. Coy & proceeded to rest billets in ARRAS.	

Army Form C. 2118.

WAR DIARY
or
INTELLIGENCE SUMMARY
(Erase heading not required.)

Instructions regarding War Diaries and Intelligence Summaries are contained in F. S. Regs., Part II. and the Staff Manual respectively. Title Pages will be prepared in manuscript.

Place	Date	Hour	Summary of Events and Information	Remarks and references to Appendices
ARRAS	25th		Company moved by motor bus from ARRAS to DUISANS. Transport proceeded independently.	
DUISANS	26th		Company moved at 1 hours notice to HABARCQ, together with 1st line Transport.	
HABARCQ	27th		Company moved by road to Cellule de LAHERLIERE to refit.	
LAHERLIERE	30th		Orders received for Company to move back to WANQUETIN on the following day.	

H.R. Dundle
Major
Comm'g 87th Machine Gun Company.

Appendix I

Copy No. 2.

87th Machine Gun Company Operation Order No. 16

In the Field. April 21st 1917.

Ref: Map: "Special Sheet" MONCHY-LE-PREUX.
1/10,000

1.) The general Advance will be continued on a date and at a Zero hour to be notified later.

2.) The objectives of ?/?/?/? ? will be as follows:—

1st Objective: (BLUE LINE)..... COPSE. O.8.b.1.2. (inclusive) — O.2 central — I.26.c.2.2.

2nd Objective: (RED LINE)... O.9.d.5.0 — O.9.b.6.5. — O.3.a.5.0 — O.3.c.2.8 — Eastern Edge of BOIS DU SART — Sandpits at I.27.d.3.4.

3.) 88th Inf. Bde. will be attacking on the right, 51st Bde. (17th Division) on the left.

1st Objective: 1/K.O.S.B. will attack on the right, 2/S.W.B. on the left.
2nd Objective: 1/R. Innis: Fus. " " " " " , 1/Borders "

4.) Machine Gun Action.

(i) There will be Two main Machine Gun Barrages, called 'A' & 'B'.

"A". A moving barrage to cover the advance of the Infantry, developing into a standing barrage to cover the consolidation of the 1st Objective. This opens at Zero on a N. & S. line from O.8 central to O.2.b.0.7, remaining on this line until Zero + 8 minutes.

At O+8 mins., O+16 mins, O+24 mins. & O+32 mins. there will be a lift of 200 yards until the final barrage line is a N. & S. line from O.9.a.0.0 to I.3.c.0.0.

"B". A protective barrage in front of 2nd Objective on a N. & S. line from O.4 central to I.31 central.

(ii) No. 3 Section O.6.3.2
Target: Valley in J.?? central. Range not to be less than 1600 yds. ...
?+?? minutes. At ?+?? ... ...

2.

final "A" Barrage line (from O3614. to I.33.c.0.6), remaining there till O+7 hours. At O+7 hours section moves up (2 guns at a time) into 1st objective (O.2 central), & carries out "B" barrage from I.34.c.0.0. to I.34.a.0.0.

(iii) No 2 Section will occupy positions about O1c.7.2. Targets: Valley in O7d — Sunken Road & ruined Mill in O8a and O8c — COPSE in O8b. Their guns will fire direct from zero hour except when masked by our own infantry. At O+32 mins. lift on to final "A" barrage line (from O9a.7.1 to O3.c.0.7.). At O+7 hours section moves up (2 guns at a time) to 1st objective (O3d) & carries out "B" barrage from O4.c.a.a. to O4.b.a.b.

(iv) No 4 Section will form up at North end of jumping off trench at Zero. They will follow 2nd wave of infantry & take up positions as follows:—
   2 guns in COPSE O2a.2.5. Target: Valley in I.32 central including KEELING COPSE.
   2 guns in a position from which they can control Valley in I.33.c. including COPSE at I.32.a.9.?
As soon as 1st Objective is consolidated, the 2 guns at COPSE O2a.2.5. will advance to a position in or in front of 1st Objective, from which they can control by direct fire the BOIS du SART.
Section will advance to 2nd Objective in rear of the Infantry (shortly after O+7 hours) & occupy positions in 2nd Objective as follows:—
   2 guns in Northern Edge of BOIS du SART, firing on HATCHETT WOOD & JIGSAW WOOD.
   1 gun in Eastern End of BOIS du SART, covering our own front.
   1 gun at Southern Edge of BOIS du SART, (about O3.b.1.2) controlling valley in O3.d.

(v) No 1 Section will occupy positions in N6.d. & will be under O.C. 86th M.G. Coy.
Targets: Valley in O9c — BOIS du SART — BOIS du SART.
When 2nd objective is consolidated, the section moves up to 1st objective (O8.c) & fires on "B" Barrage Line from O1.c central to O1.d.O.8.

(3.)

5.) The assault will be made under cover of a creeping barrage which will start 250 yards in front of our trenches at Zero.

6.) **Dump.** A Company S.A.A. dump (containing S.A.A., oil & water) is being formed tonight at O.6.3.3, and will be under the C.S.M. A local dump for No 2 Section is being formed at O.1.a.4. O.C. No 2 Section will place one man in charge of this Dump. Section Officers firing the barrage will draw sufficient S.A.A. for the barrage from these dumps to-night, & place it by each gun.

Shortly after O+7 hours the main Company Dump will be moved forward to S. end of COPSE at O.2.a.30.55, under arrangements to be made by the C.S.M.

7.) **Carrying Part.** Carrying parties will report as follows, at a time & place to be notified later:— No 1 Section 12, No 2 Section 12 men. No 3 Section 12 men. No 4 Section 16 men. S.A.A. Dump (under the C.S.M.) 10 men.

8.) Sections detailed to advance at O+7 hours to 2nd Objective will only move forward when the Section Officer is satisfied that the advance from the BLUE to the RED Line is in progress. If the advance to the RED Line has not taken place Section Officers will continue to fire on the final "A" Barrage Line.

9.) The position of Company H.Q. will be notified later.

10.) Please acknowledge.

Copies:
1 — Office
1, 3 — War Diary
4 — 27th Inf. Bde
5 — O.C. No 1 Section
6 — — 2 Section
7 — — 3 Section
8 — — 4 Section
9 — 2nd Lt Morris
10 — 2nd Lt Quinn
11 — C.S.M. White
12 — 86th M.G. Coy
13 — 88th M.G. Coy
14 — H.L.I.
15 — K.O.S.B.
16 — 1/R. Innis: Fus.
17 — 1/Border Regt

G. H. Moberly
Lieut, Capt.
27th Machine Gun

Issued at 1630

H.Q
Appendix 2

87th Infantry Brigade.

I beg to report as follows in regard to the operations of this Company on April 23rd & 24th.
On the morning of April 23rd, the disposition of guns was as follows:-

No 3 Section (4 guns) in CHATEAU WOOD O1 a 6.6
No 2 Section (4 guns) about O1 c 9.2
No 4 Section (4 guns) mobile Section on Left Flank.
No 1 Section (4 guns) (attached 86th Machine Gun Company) at N6 d 4.0

A Brigade Dump of 160,000 rounds S.A.A. and 32 petrol tins of water was established at O1 d 10.35.

MOBILE SECTION

The Mobile Section under Lieut. H.P. Leward advanced on the left flank with the 2nd wave of Infantry. The officer was wounded and two gun teams were put out of action. The remaining 2 guns worked up to the 1st Objective and took up positions about O2a 8.6 and O2a 9.3. 10 Belt Boxes per gun were collected by the N.C.O's in charge from killed and wounded carriers.

These guns engaged several targets, including a German counter attack directed against 1st K.O.S.B'rs between 1600 & 1630 on 23rd April, and remained in action until relieved on the night of the 24th.

BARRAGE SECTIONS

The remaining guns carried out the 1st part of the barrage table ('A' Barrage) in accordance with the Corps Scheme. In addition the following targets were engaged:-

By No 2 Section. (1) Parties of Germans at CAVALRY FARM at mid-day.
(2) German counter attack on right flank

at 1600.
By No 3 Section.

At 1050 orders were issued to the guns not to advance to 1st Objective, as previously ordered, and informing them that a counter attack was expected on MONCHY from the direction of PELVES. 2 more guns were placed in CHATEAU WOOD, one from No 2 Section and one salvaged by Lieut. L.H. Layne, from the Mobile Section.

At ——— 1 gun of No 2 Section with its gun team were destroyed. About 1500 No 1 Section rejoined the Company and was ordered to move at dusk to N.6.b.9.6 from which they could command Square I.31.

No 2 At 2000 orders were issued to O.C. No 2 Section to move up on gun to old front line during the night and to take charge of that gun and the 2 guns of No 4 Section already there. This gun took up a position about O2a.5.7.

On the 24th April O.C. Company attended a Conference at 86th Brigade H.Q., and received orders to support the attack of 86th Brigade on the 2nd Objective at 1600. All guns except the gun in front line were detailed to support this attack with barrage fire (orders issued to Sections as attached.)

The Company was relieved on the night of the 24th April.

GENERAL REMARKS
(1) An average of 2000 rounds S.A.A. per gun was expended on each barrage.
(2) About ——— gallons of water per gun

team (this includes drinking water & water for the gun) were used during the 2 days.

(3) The casualties in gunners of the mobile Section were as heavy as the total casualties of the other 3 Sections.

(4) A party of 50 men from the Battalions were detailed as carriers. These were allotted as follows:- 16 to mobile Section, 12 each to Nos 2 & 3 Sections, 10 to C.S.M. for moving forward the dump of S.A.A. and water. The casualties among these carriers were heavy, especially amongst those attached to the mobile Section.

(5) It was previously arranged to move forward the dump of S.A.A. & water to ARROWHEAD COPSE. This was cancelled when the attack on the 2nd objective was postponed.

RECOMMENDATIONS

(1) It is recommended that the carrying party should be increased to 62. This would enable 12 men to be attached to the 4th Section.

(2) The vulnerability of Machine Guns both on the move and in fighting at close quarters is not always sufficiently realized. Whenever possible the Machine Gun barrage should be arranged from stationary positions and a mobile Section is only required when it is impossible to protect the objective from positions in rear. On every occasion the officer in charge of the mobile Section has been either wounded or killed, and the casualties among the gunners over 50%.

It is suggested that if a continuous and dense Machine Gun fire barrage in front of the objective (1 belt per gun every 8 minutes) were kept up during the whole of the 1st day, this

(IV)

together with the Lewis Guns in the front line should be sufficient to hold up a counter attack. Machine Guns could then be pushed up at dusk with practically no casualties.

(3) It is recommended that the rate of fire for Machine Gun barrage should be
(a) During actual attack, 1 belt-box per Gun every 4 minutes. (b) For continuous barrage after the attack, 1 belt-box per Gun every 8 minutes.

(4) Owing to the impossibility of getting up hot food to the Guns during heavy fighting, an ample supply of solidified alcohol is considered very necessary.

(5) The system of taking up 3 days rations before the attack was very successful & undoubtedly saved many casualties. It is recommended that this should always be done.

SIGNED:

S.R. Burnett MAJOR.
Comg. 87th Machine Gun Coy.

COPY   **SECRET**

O.C. No 3 Section
    R.F.A.M.

V/1035   24-4-17.

(1) 86th Brigade are attacking 2nd objective this afternoon at 1600.

(2) Your 6 guns will fire as follows:-

(a) Zero to Zero + 5 minutes. KEELING COPSE and WOOD in I.32.d.95.15

(b) Zero + 5 minutes to Zero + 10 minutes. Western edge of BOIS DU SART from O.3.a.5.4 to O.3.b.1.0.

(c) Zero + 10 minutes to Zero + 15 minutes. Eastern edge of BOIS DU SART from O.4.a.4.9 to O.4.a.3.2.

(d) Zero + 15 minutes to Zero + 30 mins. "B" Barrage line from I.34.a.2.2 to O.4.b.2.2.

(e) Zero + 30 mins. Cease fire.

In addition to the above targets you will engage any other suitable targets that may appear. For this purpose you will establish a post to watch events.

Signed: G.H. Moberly
    Lieut & Capt.
    R.F.A.M.

O.C. No 1 Section   **SECRET**
    R.F.A.M.

V/1235   24-4-17.

1. 86th Brigade are attacking 2nd objective at 1600 this afternoon.

2. Your guns will fire as follows:-

(a) Zero to Zero + 5 minutes: CARTRIDGE TRENCH ~~N.W.~~ ~~BOIS DU SART~~ from I.32.b.25.00 to 32.b.2.6.

(b) Zero + 5 minutes to Zero + 10 minutes: N.W. edge of BOIS DU SART from I.33.d.1.3 to O.3.a.40.80

(c) Zero + 10 minutes to Zero + 15 mins: from road junction I.33.d.6.4 to I.34.c.0.0.

(d) At Zero + 15 minutes, cease fire.

In addition to the above targets you will fire on any other good targets which may appear.

Signed: G.H. Moberly
    Lieut & Capt.
    R.F.A.M.

SECRET.   COPY   COPY XI

29th Division Instructions No. 3.

20th April 1917.

1. In order to fully utilise the fire power of the Brigade Machine Gun Companies the following scheme will be carried out during the operations on the 23rd instant.

2. There will be two main barrages, which will be referred to through this scheme as **A** and **B**.

A. A moving barrage to cover the advance of the Infantry, developing into a standing barrage to cover the consolidation of the first objective. To open on a N. and S. line from O.8. central to O.2.b.0.7. at zero, remaining on this line until zero plus 8 minutes. At O plus 8 mins, O plus 16 minutes, O plus 24 minutes, O plus 32 minutes, there will be a lift of 200 yards until the final barrage line is a N. and S. line from O.9.a.6.0. to I.33.c.0.6.

B. A protective barrage in front of the second objective on a N and S. line from O.10. central to I.34. central.

3. The grouping of guns and action will be as follows:—

88th Machine Gun Company.

(1) A Group of 12 guns at N.12.b.8.8. To open fire at zero & carry out the barrage A, remaining on the final barrage line of the first objective until O plus 7 hours.

At O plus 6 hours, however, 6 guns of this group move forward to the Sunken Road about O.8.c. to O.7.b. and carry out barrage **B.** from O.10. central to O.4.d.0.5.

The other 6 Guns remain on the final barrage of the first objective until O plus 7 hours. They then cease fire and move up to positions in the first objective and will be prepared to open on to barrage B. should they be required, owing to casualties placing other Guns, detailed for this purpose, out of action.

(2) A group of four Mobile Guns. To be in the Southern End of jumping off trench at zero. To follow the second wave of Infantry and take up a position about O.8 central and to control by direct fire the road & houses in O.14.a. When not masked by our Infantry at O. plus 7 hours, to advance to second objective in rear of Infantry and engage such targets as may appear.

87th Machine Gun Company.
(1) A Group of 4 Guns about O.1.b.3.3. Target, Valley in 1.33.c central. Range not less than 1500 yards. To fire from Zero to O. plus 32 minutes. At O plus 32 minutes to lift 200 yards remaining on final barrage line of 1st Objective until O plus 7 hours, when group ceases fire and moves up into 1st Objective and carries out barrage B from 1.34.d.0.0. to 1.34.b.0.0.

(2) A Group of 4 Guns about O.1.c.9.2. Target, Valley in 1.33.c - Sunken Road and ruined mill in O.8.a. and c: - Copse in O.8.b. to fire direct when not masked by our Infantry, from Zero. At O plus 32 minutes to lift on to final barrage line of 1st Objective. To cease fire at O.plus 7 hours & then move up to 1st Objective and carry out barrage B. from O.10.central to O.4.d.0.5.

(3) A Group of 4 Mobile Guns. To be in northern end of jumping Off trench at Zero. To follow second wave of Infantry and take up a position about the Copse O.2.a.2.0. Two Guns to control by direct fire the Valley in 1.32. and 2 guns the Valley in 1.33.c when not masked by our Infantry.

As soon after the capture of the first objective to work forward as close to our artillery standing barrage as possible and to control by direct fire the Valley in 1.33.c. central and the BOIS-du SART.

These Guns advance to 2nd Objective in rear of Infantry and engage such targets as may appear.

86th M G Coy: and 87th M G Coy

A group of 8 guns, 4 of 86th M G Coy and 4 of 87th M G Coy under O.C 86th M G Coy at about H.6.d.target, Valley O.9.c. :- BOIS du VERT — BOIS-du-SART to cease fire at O plus 7 hours. The 4 Guns of 87th Machine Gun Company then move up to 1st Objective and reinforce barrage B line as required.

86th Machine Gun Company.
(1) A Group of 4 Guns referred to in previous para:. Remainder of guns in Reserve — 8 of these Guns to move up after capture of 1st Objective to MONCHY and take over

defences in positions vacated by 87th M.G. Coy.

4. — For the above scheme it is roughly estimated that each gun will require 10 boxes S.A.A. Each Brigade will be responsible for dumping this together with tins of water as far forward as possible before operations commence.

A carrying party of 50 Infantry should be attached to the 87th Machine Gun Company & to the 88th Machine Gun Company. for carrying forward S.A.A. etc:- after the operations commence.

5. Attached is a table for Machine Gun fire orders, copies of which, if required, can be obtained on application to these Headquarters.

6. Mobile Machine Guns detailed to accompany the Infantry to the 2nd Objective must keep their Belt-Boxes full for the advance from the BLUE to the RED Line.

7. The Guns detailed to advance at O. plus 7 hours to the 1st Objective will only move forward when the Officer in charge has satisfied himself that the advance from the BLUE to the RED Line has commenced.

8. Officers Commanding Machine Gun Groups must keep in touch with the situation and be prepared to cover the BLUE line, should for any reason the advance to the RED line not take place.

9. ACKNOWLEDGE by Wire

Signed — C. Fuller
Lieut: Col: G.S.,
29th Division

Issued at 12 noon.

Copies
1 — 5   General Staff
6 — 10   86th Brigade
11 — 15 87th   "
16 — 20 88th   "
21   17th Division
22   15 —
23   6th Corps M.G.O.
24   6th Corps "G"

Vol/2

CONFIDENTIAL

War Diary

of

87th Machine Gun Company

from 1st May 1917 to 31st May 1917.

VOLUME XII

WAR DIARY or INTELLIGENCE SUMMARY

Army Form C. 2118.

Place	Date	Hour	Summary of Events and Information	Remarks and references to Appendices
In the Field	May 1st		Company marched with Transport to WANQUETIN.	
	2nd		Company marched with Transport to ARRAS	
	3rd		Company proceeded to OBSERVATION HILL in Reserve for the general attack along the front. 1 officer 12 O.R. Taken on Strength of Company.	
	4th		Company returned from Reserve Line to ARRAS.	
	7th		Company marched with Transport to Huts in DUISANS No 1 Camp	
	13th		Company marched from DUISANS to the Trenches (MONCHY Sector), relieving 8th 9th & 76th M.G. Companies. 1 officer Evacuated Sick. 1 O.R. (Struck off Strength)	
	14th		1 machine gun blown up by shell fire. — 3 O.R. Killed 1 O.R. Wounded.	
	16th		Casualties:- 1 O.R. Killed. 1 O.R. Wounded	
	18th		Company Operation Order No 17 issued (see appendix I.)	
	19th		87th Infy Brigade attacked the German Trenches at 9 pm. The attack was held up by hostile machine gun & rifle fire and no ground was gained. In consequence the 4th machine guns which had been detailed to go forward remained in their former positions with the exception of one gun in SHRAPNEL TR. which went forward under Lieut. L.K. MORRIS to TWIN TRENCH (front line). This was found to be held very lightly by the infantry owing to casualties, and as a German counter attack was expected the machine gun was placed in front of TWIN COPSES to cover our own front line. S.A.A. expended on M.G. barrage by 10 machine guns during and after the attack 31,000 rounds. On this occasion the arrangement of machine guns going forward to objective (if captured) 2 hours after zero instead of with the infantry proved successful, not one casualty being incurred. If guns had gone forward with Infantry several guns would undoubtedly have been put out of action.	
	20th		Company (less 3 guns) relieved from the trenches by the 86th Machine Gun Company & proceeded to rest in ARRAS.	

Army Form C.-2118.

WAR DIARY
or
INTELLIGENCE SUMMARY

(Erase heading not required.)

Instructions regarding War Diaries and Intelligence Summaries are contained in F. S. Regs., Part II. and the Staff Manual respectively. Title Pages will be prepared in manuscript.

Place	Date	Hour	Summary of Events and Information	Remarks and references to Appendices
In the Field	21st May		Remaining 3 Guns relieved by 86th Machine Gun Company & returned to ARRAS. 1 O.R. Wounded	
	22nd		3 O.R. Evacuated Sick out of Divisional Area. 1 O.R. Transferred to R.E. Railway Transportation BOULOGNE (Struck off Strength of Company)	
	23rd		2 O.R. Evacuated Sick out of Divisional Area	
	24th		8 O.R. — do — do —	
	26th		1 O.R. — do — do —	
	28th		Lieut S. P. ASHTON taken on Strength of Company. Nos 1, 2 & 4 Sections proceeded to the Trenches & came under the orders of O.C. 86th Machine Gun Company in preparation for covering a local attack by 86th Brigade of the following evening. 1 O.R. Killed 3 O.R. Wounded	
	29th		No. 3 Section remained with Company Headquarters at ARRAS. Operations by 86th Brigade postponed.	
	30th		8 guns of Company under the Officer Commanding 86th Machine Gun Company co-operated in an attack on HOOK T'S	
	31		Company relieved the 86th Machine Gun Company in the Trenches. No. 1 Section in SHRAPNEL T'R. No. 2 Section (3 guns) TWIN (5 guns) in MONCHY DEFENCES, No. 3 Section, 4 Strong points in rear of MONCHY, No. 4 Section TRENCH (2 guns) - ORCHARD T.R.	

J C Browning
Lieut
for O.C. 87th Machine Gun Company.

(Appendix I)   COPY No 2.

SECRET

87th Machine Gun Company Operation Order No 16.

May 18. 1917

(1) On May 19th, at a Zero hour, to be notified later, the 29th. Division has been ordered to capture INFANTRY HILL and the BOIS DES AUBEPINES in conjunction with the 56th. Division (on the right), who will cooperate and occupy those parts of LONG TRENCH & HOOK TRENCH which lie within their area.

(2) The 87th Infantry Brigade will attack objectives shown in RED & BLUE in attached map.   (NO MAP ATTACHED)

(3) The attack will take place under the cover of an intense artillery barrage, which will open at Zero on the Red Line. It will lift at Zero + 5 minutes and advance at the rate of 100 yds. in 2 mins. to the Blue Line, from which it will lift at Zero + 10 minutes.

(4) Order of Battle. The attack will be carried out by the 1st R. Innis Fus. on the right & 1st Border Regt. on the left.

(5) Stray Points. Stray points will be dug at the following places. O.2.d.10.2½, O.3.c.2½.6, O.2.d.10.9, O.2.b.8.4½, O.2.b.6.9, I.32.d.1.0, I.32.c.9.3, I.32.c.9.4., I.32.c.2.5,

(6) Machine Gun Action (a) No 1 Section will support the attack as follows. 2 CHATEAU guns will open rapid fire at Zero on the square contained by the points O.3.a.5.1., O.3.b.1.2., O.3.d.2.5, O.3.c.6.6., Two guns at O.1.c.85.85, will open rapid fire at Zero from O.3.c.7.1 to O.9.a.7.5.

(b) No 2 Section will support the attack as follows:- 2 guns in SHRAPNEL TRENCH at O.2.c.15.15 and O.2.c.3.6. will go forward to the second objective to O.2.d.95.20 and O.2.d.95.80. respectively. They will, as far as possible choose a quiet moment to move forward, but must start not later than Zero + 2 hours.

2 guns in ~~each~~ EAST TRENCH will open rapid fire at Zero from O.3.c.6.7 to O.3.c.7.0. At midnight these two guns will move to positions in SHRAPNEL TRENCH

(c) No 3 Section will support the attack as follows:- The 2 guns in TWIN TRENCH and SHRAPNEL TRENCH will go forward to second objective to I.32.c.60.05 and O.2.b.95.40. respectively

They will as far as possible, choose a quiet moment to go forward, but must start not later than Zero + 2 hours.

The gun at O.1.b.5.1 will open rapid fire at Zero from O3.c.6.7 to O3.c.6.3. The gun in SNAFFLE TRENCH will open rapid fire at Zero on the part of DEVILS TRENCH North of BIT LANE (except where prevented by our own troops)

(d) No 4 Section will support the attack as follows. The 2 guns in HUSSAR LANE will open rapid fire at Zero on the square contained by the following points O.3.a.5.1 O.3.b.1.2. O3.d.2.5. O3.c.6.6

The 2 guns in VINE LANE (in O.7.b.3.9) will open rapid fire at Zero from O.9.a.6.5 to O.9.a.6.0. At 12 midnight these guns will move forward to positions in SHRAPNEL TRENCH

All the above guns, which open rapid fire at Zero, will continue rapid fire till Zero + 1½ hours. They will then fire intermittently for the remainder of the night.

(7) <u>Carrying Parties</u>. Carrying parties will report as follows:

(I) From 1st Border Regiment (a) 8 men to report to gun in TWIN TRENCH at O2.a.6.6 at 6pm on 19th inst.

(b) 8 men to report to LIEUT. MORRIS at junction of SHRAPNEL and LID TRENCHES at 6pm on 19th inst.

(II) From 1st R. Innis Fus. (a) 8 men to report to LIEUT. NOLAN at junction of SHRAPNEL and CANISTER TRENCHES at 6pm 19th inst.

(b) 8 men to report to LIEUT. NOLAN at junction of SHRAPNEL TRENCH and RIGHT COMMUNICATION TRENCH (forward part of GRAPE TRENCH) at O.2.c.2.0 at 6pm 19th inst.

(8) <u>Communication trenches</u>. Communication trenches will be dug from O.2.d.1.3 to O.2.d.9.3 and from O.2. until to O.2.b.6.0

(9) There will be an advanced Dressing Station at N.5.a.6.3

(10) Watches will be synchronized at 9.30 a.m. and 5.30 p.m. on 19th inst.

11) Please acknowledge.

Issued at 2100

Copies 1. - Office
2. - ⎱ War diary
3. - ⎰
4. - OC No 1 Section
5. - OC No 2 Section
6. - OC No 3 Section
7. - OC No 4 Section
8. - 87th Infantry Brigade
9. - D.M.G.O
10. - 1st R. Innis Fus
11. - 1st Border Regt
12. - 2nd S.W.B

JH Nobatty
Lieut Adjt
87th Machine Gun Coy

SECRET. ✓   Copy N° 10

87th Machine Gun Company Operation Order N° 16

May 18th 1917

Ref: map attached

1) On May 19th at a Zero hour to be notified later, the 29th Divn have been ordered to capture INFANTRY HILL and the BOIS DES AUBEPINES in conjunction with the 56th Division (on the right) who will cooperate and occupy those parts of LONG TRENCH & HOOK TRENCH which lie within their area.

2) The 87th Brigade will attack objectives shown in Red & Blue in attached map.

3) The attack will take place under cover of an intense Artillery Barrage which will open at zero on the Red Line. It will lift at zero + 5 mins and advance at the rate of 100 yards in 2 mins: to the Blue line, from which it will lift at zero + 10 mins.

4) Order of Battle The attack will be carried out by 1st R. Innis Fus on the right, & 1st Border Regt on the left.

5) Strong Points Strong points will be dug at the following places:-
O.2.d.10.2½, O.3.c.2½.6, O.2.d.10.9, O.2.b.8.4½, O.2.b.6.9.
I.32.d.1.0, I.32.c.7.3, I.32.c.3.4, I.32.c.2.5.

6) Machine Gun Action
   a) N° 1 Section will support the attack as follows:-
2 CHATEAU Guns will open rapid fire at zero on the square contained by the following points:- O.3.a.5.1, O.3.b.1.2, O.3.d.2.5, O.3.c.6.6.
2 Guns at O.1.c.85.85 will open rapid fire at zero from O.3.c.7.1 to O.9.a.7.5.

   b) N° 2 Section will support the attack as follows:-
The 2 Guns in SHRAPNEL TRENCH at O.2.c.15.15 and O.2.c.3.6 will go forward to the 2nd Objective to O.2.d.95.20 and O.2.d.95.80 respectively. They will as far as possible choose a quiet moment to move forward, but must start not later than zero + 2 hours.
The 2 guns in EAST TRENCH will open rapid fire at zero from O.3.c.6.7. to O.3.c.7.0. At midnight these 2 guns will move to positions in SHRAPNEL TRENCH.

   c) N° 3 Section will support the attack as follows:-
The 2 guns in TWIN TRENCH and SHRAPNEL TRENCH will go forward to 2nd Objective to I.32.c.60.05 and O.2.b.75.40 respectively
They will as far as possible choose a quiet moment to go forward but must start not later than zero plus 2 hours.
The gun at O.1.b.5.1 will open rapid fire at zero from O.3.c.6.7 to

O.3.c.6.3. The gun in SNAFFLE TRENCH will open rapid fire at zero on the part of DEVIL'S TRENCH North of BIT LANE (except where prevented by our own troops.)

d) No 4 Section will support the attack as follows:—

The 2 guns in HUSSAR LANE will open rapid fire at zero on the square formed by the following points:— O.3.a.5.1., O.3.b.1.2., O.3.d.2.5., O.3.c.6.6.

The two guns in VINE LANE (O.7.b.3.9.) will open rapid fire at zero from O.9.a.6.5. to O.9.a.6.0. At 12 midnight these guns will move forward to positions in SHRAPNEL TRENCH

All the above guns which open rapid fire at zero will continue rapid fire till zero + 1½ hours. They will then fire intermittently for the remainder of the night.

7) **Carrying Parties** Carrying parties will report as follows.

I. From 1st Border Regt (a) 8 men to report to gun in TWIN TRENCH at O.2.a.6.6. at 6pm on 19th inst:

(b) 8 men to report to Lt Morris at junction of SHRAPNEL & LID TRENCHES at 6pm on 19th inst:

II From 1st R. Innis: Fus (a) 8 men to report to Lt NOLAN at junction of SHRAPNEL & CANISTER TRENCHES at 6pm on 19th inst:

(b) 8 men to report to Lt NOLAN at junction of SHRAPNEL TR and night communication trench (forward part of GRAPE TR) at O.2.c.2.0 at 6pm, 19th inst:

8) **Communication Trenches** — Communication Trenches will be dug from O.2.d.1.3. to O.2.d.9.3. and from O.2 central to O.2.b.6.0.

9) There will be an advanced Dressing Station at H.5.a.6.3.

10) Watches will be synchronized at 9.30 AM and 5.30 pm on 19th inst

11) Please acknowledge.

Issued at 2100

Copies
1. — Office
2, 3. — War Diary
4 — O.C. No 1 Section
5 — O.C. No 2 "
6 — O.C. No 3 "
7 — O.C. No 4 "
8 — 87th Infty Brigade
9 — D.M.G.O.
10 — 1st R. Innis. Fus
11 — 1st Border Regt
12 — 2 S.W.B.

J H Moberly
Lieut & Adjt
87th Machine Gun Coy

NEALM

CONFIDENTIAL

WAR DIARY

of

the

87th Machine Gun Company

for

1st June 1917 to 30th June 1917.

(VOLUME 13)

WAR DIARY or INTELLIGENCE SUMMARY

Army Form C. 2118.

Place	Date	Hour	Summary of Events and Information	Remarks and references to Appendices
In the Field	June 3rd		1 Other Rank Evacuated Sick out of Divisional Area.	
	4th		3 " " Transferred from 88th Machine Gun Company.	
	5th		1 " " Evacuated Sick out of Divisional Area. — Company Transport proceeded to FIENVILLERS by Road	
	6th		Company proceeded to FIENVILLERS by Train from ARRAS STATION arriving at BELLEU about 2.30 pm. Company Transport arrived at FIENVILLERS about 11.0 am. — 3 O.R. Taken on Strength of Coy from Base. 2 O.R. Evacuated Sick out of Divisional Area.	
	7th		24 Other Ranks Taken on Strength of Company from Base.	
	10th		2 O.Ranks Evacuated Sick out of Divisional Area.	
	11th		1 O.R. Taken on Strength of Coy from Hospital	
	12th		1 O.R. " " do " " do	
	14th		3 O.R. " " do " " from Base	
	15th		1 O.R. Evacuated Sick out of Divisional Area	
	18th		1 O.R. Taken on Strength of Coy from Hospital	
	20th		1 O.R. Evacuated Sick out of Divisional Area	
	21st		Company marched with Transport from FIENVILLERS to BOULLENS Stn. Entrained at 3.19, arriving about 9.20 pm. Company with Transport proceeded to camp at HOPOUTRE, POPERINGHE via CROMBEKE.	
	28th		1 Other Rank Evacuated Sick out of Divisional Area. Nos. 1, 2 and Headquarters Sections proceeded to the line (BRIELEN Sector) followed by Nos. 3 & 4 Sections and relieved the 113th Mn. G. Company. Company Headquarters established on Canal Bank. No. 1 Section in Left Sector No. 3 Section supplied 1 Team to Right Sector No. 2 " " Right Sector	

Army Form C. 2118.

WAR DIARY
or
INTELLIGENCE SUMMARY
(Erase heading not required.)

Place	Date	Hour	Summary of Events and Information	Remarks and references to Appendices
In the Field	28th June		No. 3 Section less 1 Team with Section in reserve at Company Headquarters. No. 4 Section firing at night with 4 guns. No. 3 Section supplying working party. Appendix I attached :— Lessons Learned during month of May 1917	

J.C. Watson Lieut & Adjt
87th Machine Gun Company

THIRD ARMY — COPY — APPENDIX I

With reference to Third Army letter No. G.26/93, dated 27th. March 1917, I beg to report as follows:-

A. TACTICAL LESSONS

1) **Rate of fire in Machine Gun Barrage.**

It has been found that the best rate of fire for a Machine Gun barrage is (a) During actual attack an average of one belt per gun every five minutes (b) for a continuous barrage after the attack one belt every twelve minutes. A more intensive fire is incompatible with keeping the gun in action for a continuous period.

2) **Carrying Parties**

It has been found that a carrying party of 60 men from the Infantry is necessary for a Machine Gun Company in an attack. This enables all guns to get forward together with a minimum amount of belt boxes and a Company dump of reserve SAA to be gradually moved forward to a previously selected place in front of our lines.

3) **Machine Guns in Attack**
Inadvisibility of Advancing with Infantry

The vulnerability of machine guns both on the move and in fighting at close quarters, is not always sufficiently realised. Whenever possible, the machine gun barrage should be arranged for stationary positions and a mobile section is only required when it is impossible to protect the objective from positions in the rear. On every occasion the officer in command of the mobile section has either been killed or wounded and the casualties among the gunners over 50%. It is suggested that if a continuous and dense machine gun barrage in front of the objective were kept up during the whole of the first day, this together with the Lewis Guns in the front line, should be sufficient to hold up counter-attacks.

Machine Guns could then be pushed up to the objective at dusk with practically no casualties, or, as an alternative, they could be sent forward at any moment the section officer considers the conditions suitable, but within a previously stated period from the time of assault, say, two hours.

4/ **Use of O.P's and Harassing fire by machine guns**

It is suggested that one group of guns, (say one section) sited so that they can open fire by day, and that these guns be connected by telephone to a special machine gun O.P. The guns should be provided with artillery range cards and should be ready to open fire immediately on any target indicated from that O.P.

B **TECHNICAL LESSONS**

1/ It is recommended that the traversing dial be graduated from 0° to 360°, instead of the present arrangement, which is liable to lead to confusion.

2/ At least two, & if possible, four, clinometers per section are required.

3/ It is considered that a small type of night firing box fitted with an electric lamp, operated from the gun, would be far preferable to the old siege lamp.

(Signed) H.R. Burrill

Major
Comm'g &c M Gun Co.

CONFIDENTIAL.

WAR DIARY

of the

87th Machine Gun Company.

for

1st July 1917 to 31st July 1917

(VOLUME XIV)

Army Form C. 2118.

WAR DIARY
or
INTELLIGENCE SUMMARY.
(Erase heading not required.)

Instructions regarding War Diaries and Intelligence Summaries are contained in F. S. Regs., Part II. and the Staff Manual respectively. Title pages will be prepared in manuscript.

Place	Date	Hour	Summary of Events and Information	Remarks and references to Appendices
YPRES (Canal Bank)	July 1		No 3 Section relieved No 1 Section. No 1 Section relieved No 2 Section	
"	"		No 2 Section remaining at Company Headquarters on Canal Bank	
"	"		1 O.R. taken on strength of Company from Base. 1 O.R. evacuated sick out of area.	
"	July 2		Anti-aircraft mountings erected on CANAL BANK and manned by No 2 Section	
"	3		1 O.R. killed in action & 1 O.R. wounded in action	
"	4		1 O.R. rejoined Company from Hospital. 1 Officer & 2 O.R. wounded in action (1 O.R. died of wounds)	
"	5		1 Officer & 9 O.R. proceeded to Fifth Army Rest Camp. 1 O.R. wounded in action	
"	6		Company relieved by 86th Machine Gun Company, marched to W Camp, CROMBEKE and (under canvas)	
"	7		No 1 Section proceeded to HARINGHE on anti-aircraft duty. 11 O.R. taken on strength of Company from Base	
"	8		1 O.R. taken on strength of Company from Base	

Army Form C. 2118.

WAR DIARY
or
INTELLIGENCE SUMMARY.

(Erase heading not required.)

Instructions regarding War Diaries and Intelligence Summaries are contained in F. S. Regs., Part II. and the Staff Manual respectively. Title pages will be prepared in manuscript.

Place	Date	Hour	Summary of Events and Information	Remarks and references to Appendices
N^a CROMBEKE	July 9/17		1 Officer taken on strength of Company from Base	
	-11		2 O.R. " " " " " "	
	-12		No 2 Section proceeded to "L" defences and No 3 Section to DRAGON CAMP anti-aircraft positions	
	-13		Company Headquarters with transport and No 4 Section proceeded to PRAED CAMP (PROVEN 2 area)	
	-14		No 3 Section evacuated "L" defences and took up positions in "Y" Lines, Guards area. No 4 Section proceeded to "X" Line	
	-15		No 1 Section evacuated anti-aircraft positions at HARINGHE and returned to Company Headquarters	
	-16		Lieut O.P. ASHTON wounded in action	
	-17		Company Headquarters and transport removed to DRAGON CAMP	
	-18		1 O.R. returned to Company from Hospital	
	-20		Company relieved by 113 & 217th Machine Gun Companies, returned to PRAED CAMP (PROVEN 2 area)	
	-23		Major H.R. BURRELL evacuated to Machine Gun Training Centre	

Army Form C. 2118.

WAR DIARY
or
INTELLIGENCE SUMMARY.
(Erase heading not required.)

Place	Date	Hour	Summary of Events and Information	Remarks and references to Appendices
FRAED CAMP	[illegible]		1 Officer & O.R. taken on strength of Company from Base	
	-26		1 Officer " " " " from Hospital	
	-29		1 O.R. evacuated to U.K. on munitions	
	-30		Company marched with transport to FOREST CAMP, Copy Received	Appendices No I
			Preliminary Operation Order No 17 issued	attached

J Mosely
Lieut. comm?
87th Machine Gun Coy.

Copy No. 1

87th Machine Gun Company Operation Order
(Preliminary) No. 7
(Appendix No. 1)

In the Field
30th July 1917

1. **General**

(a) XIV Corps in conjunction with troops on N and S, will attack the enemy on a date and at an hour to be notified later. 29th Division will be in Corps Reserve in rear of the Guards Division. 38th Division will be attacking on right of Guards and the French on left.

(b) <u>Boundaries</u>:- of Guards Division are as follows. <u>S</u>. From Canal Bank at B.12.d.5½, to C.1.d.1.6, thence along N. side of Railway. <u>N</u>. From Canal Bank at B.5.d.9½.9. to T.30.d.4½.4 to U.21.a.2.9½.

(c) <u>Objectives</u> are as follows:- Blue Line T.30.c.8.1, U.25.c.5.0, C.1.a.2½.6, C.1.a.8.0, C.8.a.8.2½. (Leave Blue Line at Zero + 0140)

Black Line T.24.c.2½.6., C.2.a.5.0., C.9.a.4.7 (Leave at Zero + 0320) Green Line U.19.c.2.0 U.27.c.5½.6., C.4.a.1.3, (Leave at Zero + 0500) Dotted Green Line T.20.c.8.5, U.21.d.3.6, U.28.a.1.9

Red Line U.20.b.4.7, U.16.c.6.6, U.24.a.0.1, U.24.c.4.0. Main Objective of first days operations will be Green Line. The Eastern Bank of the Steenbeke will also be consolidated by Guards Division.

2. **Traffic**

(1) 48 mats will be placed across the Canal and these will be supplemented by at least 16 petrol tin float bridges to take infantry in file. These bridges will be numbered 1 to 16 from right to left.

(2) BOESINGHE and CACTUS Pontoon bridges are reserved for Artillery wheeled traffic. CRAPOUILLOT Bridge is reserved for infantry "up" traffic, including pack animals and transport.

(3) Dumps will be established as follows:-
S.A.A. and GRENADES M.B.16.a.5.9 and B.10.c.8.1.
RATIONS & WATER M.B.16.a.5.9 and B.11.a.5.5
R.E. STORES AT JOYEUSE FARM and B.11.c.9.9

(4) MEDICAL Advance dressing stations are situated at

OLD MILL (B.15.a.1.5) and in main street, BOESINGHE village, also walking wounded post in BLEVET FARM (B.10.c.3.4)

(5) Runners.. All runners will carry their messages in top right hand pocket of their jacket.

(6) Officers Equipment., All officers will wear the same clothes as their men and will carry compasses.

(7) Rations etc:- Each man will carry one day's rations + Emergency Rations + unexpended portion of days rations. Two sandbags per man will also be carried.

(8) Water
  (i) Tours's water points for men will be established in (a) East Bank of Canal (1 main being taken over each bridge)
    (b) LANGEMARCK
    (c) HUDDLESTONE ROAD and near LIÈVRE CABARET
  (ii) Forward water points for horses will be established at
    (a) ELVERDINGHE CHATEAU
    (b) HULLS FARM
    (c) BOESINGHE CHATEAU

(9) Prisoners. A Divisional collecting station will be established at (B.10.d.5.9).
    All ranks are warned against taking Pocket Books containing documents or loose letters and post cards, from prisoners or dead and returning them as souvenirs

10. S.O.S. signal will be a coloured Rifle Grenade bursting into 2 Red & 2 Green lights. No other light signals will be shown, except flares showing positions of Infantry to Contact Patrols.

Issued at......
Copies 1 & 2. War Diary.
Copy. 3. Officer
  " 4 Lieut. Tarrant
  " 5 "   Downes
  " 6 "   Page
  " 7 "   Brunt
  " 8 "/" Richard
  " 9 "/" Morris
  " 10
  " 11

Signed H C Randall
Lieut and Adjt.
87th Machine Gun Coy

CONFIDENTIAL

WAR DIARY

OF

87TH MACHINE GUN COMPANY

FROM 1ST AUGUST 1917 TO 31ST AUGUST 1917

VOLUME XV

Army Form C. 2118.

WAR DIARY
or
INTELLIGENCE SUMMARY
(Erase heading not required.)

Instructions regarding War Diaries and Intelligence Summaries are contained in F. S. Regs., Part II. and the Staff Manual respectively. Title pages will be prepared in manuscript.

Place	Date	Hour	Summary of Events and Information	Remarks and references to Appendices
In the field	Aug. 1st		Lieut B. GREEN taken on strength and assumed command of Company	
	2nd		Company inspected by 56th Machine Gun Company and detrained to PROVEN? Area	
		6A.	2 O.R. taken on strength of the Company from Base	
		9A.	Company and transport proceeded to FOREST Camp in reserve	
			Company less O.R. and transport proceeded to support line infront of BOESINGHE for barrage fire. Advanced Company H.Q. established in WOODHOUSE	
		9A.	1 O.R. Wounded in Action	
		10A.	Nos. 1 and 2 Sections returned to Company O.R. in FOREST Camp for rest	
			1 O.R. wounded in action 1 O.R. evacuated sick out of Divisional Area	
		11A.	1 O.R. wounded in action	
		12A.	1 O.R. wounded in action	
		13A.	6 O.R. taken on strength of Company from Base	
		14A.	Operation Order No. 18 issued (Appendix I) 2 O.R. wounded in action	See App I
		15A.	No 2 Section proceeded to join 1st BORDER REGT (in camp) to which it was to be attached for forthcoming operations. Two guns of No 2 Section	

WAR DIARY
INTELLIGENCE SUMMARY.
(Erase heading not required.)

Army Form C. 2118.

Place	Date	Hour	Summary of Events and Information	Remarks and references to Appendices
In the Field	Aug 15th		Joined 1st K.O.S.B. Bn (in the line) and remaining two guns of No 1 Section joined 2nd S.W.B's (in the line). Remaining eight guns took up barrage positions specially prepared for operations on 16th inst. 1 Officer, Lieut V.J.H. BRUNT wounded in action, 1 O.R. evacuated sick out of Divisional Area.	
	16th		General attack delivered at 4.45 a.m. Nos. 3 & 4 Sections fired barrage from Zero to Zero + 40 minutes and then moved forward about 600 yards to previously prepared positions from which fresh barrage was fired from Zero + 1.40 to Zero + 3.10 (see Appendix I). No 2 Section, under Lieut S.I. PAGE, attached to 1st BORDER REGT) did not move forward till after daylight. Great difficulty was experienced in getting the guns etc. forward over the marshy ground between the STEENBEEK and the BROENBEEK. All four guns eventually arrived in final objective with only one casualty and took up positions there. Several casualties caused by our own artillery S.O.S. barrage falling on final objective. Other guns of No 1 Section, under Lieut S. RICHARD) attached to 1st K.O.S.B. went forward at dawn and took up positions in Strong-points in final objective (BLUE LINE). The remaining	See App. I

Army Form C. 2118.

WAR DIARY
INTELLIGENCE SUMMARY.
(Erase heading not required.)

Instructions regarding War Diaries and Intelligence Summaries are contained in F. S. Regs., Part II. and the Staff Manual respectively. Title pages will be prepared in manuscript.

Place	Date	Hour	Summary of Events and Information	Remarks and references to Appendices
In the field	Aug 16th		Two guns of No. 1 Section (under No. 10485 Cpl. ROUTLEDGE. T. R.) attacks to 2nd S.W.B's went forward on the left and took up positions in final objective of 2nd S.W.B's (GREEN LINE). The four guns of No. 2 Section were relieved at night by 88th M.G.Coy. Remaining twelve guns of the Company evacuated their positions the whole Company returned to FOREST CAMP. 4 O.R. killed in action, 13 O.R. wounded in action.	
	17th		Congratulatory messages received from XIV Corps and 1st BORDER REGT. (See Appendix II) 1 O.R. taken on strength of Company from Base.	See App II
	19th		2 O.R. evacuated sick out of Divisional Area	
	20th		1 O.R. taken on strength of Company from Base	
	21st		Company relieved 14 guns of Sgt. F. M.G. Coy in front line system, four guns being placed in left sector in the vicinity of MONTMIRAIL FARM, five guns in the centre and five guns along the railway protecting the right flank in case of LANGEMARCK being lost. 2 O.R. evacuated sick out of Divisional area	
	22nd		1 O.R. wounded by shellfire.	

WAR DIARY
INTELLIGENCE SUMMARY

Army Form C. 2118.

Place	Date	Hour	Summary of Events and Information	Remarks and references to Appendices
In the field	Aug 23rd		Hostile aeroplanes flying very low over our lines were engaged by machine guns without success. 1 O.R. taken on strength of Company from Base.	
	24th		1,000 rounds S.A.A. fired at hostile aeroplanes flying very low over our lines but without apparent result. Four guns in left sector were relieved by four guns of Sgt. M.G.Cy. which came under orders of O.C. 87th M.G.Cy. Two guns (one in centre and one in right sector) were withdrawn at dusk leaving only twelve guns in front line system. 1 O.R. taken on strength of Company from Base.	
	25th		1 O.R. rejoined Company from Hospital.	
	26th		1 O.R. evacuated sick out of Personal Area, 1 O.R. taken on strength of Company from Base.	
	27th		1 O.R. evacuated sick out of Personal Area.	Appendix I
	28th		Company marched from FOREST CAMP to PLAISTOW CAMP	Appendix II attached
	29th		Company marched from PLAISTOW CAMP to PEGWELL CAMP L.o.R.	
			Taken on strength of Company from Base.	

Pt Hurdby/Lieut

Comm.g 87th Machine Gun Cy

APPENDIX I

8th Machine Gun Company Operation Order No. 18

Copy No. 2.
To Field
" ET

August 14th 1917

Reference Maps. Special Sheets :- LANGEMARCK ⅒₀₀₀ BROENBEEK ⅒₀₀₀
BIXSCHOOTE ⅒₀₀₀

General. The attack on the Corps front in conjunction with troops on IV & V Corps will be continued on a day and at an hour to be notified later.
59th Infantry Brigade will attack on the left of the Divisional front. 88th Infantry Brigade will be on the right and 8th French Regiment on the left.

(2) **Boundaries:-** Divisional boundaries will be a straight line between U.15. central and U.20 central on the left, and the railway on the right. Boundary between Brigades will be a straight line between ROYAL FARM and CANIVES FARM.

(3) **Disposition of Machine Guns** 8 guns (Nos. 3 & 4 Sections) of the 8th M.G. Company will be firing a barrage during the attack, and 8 guns (Nos. 1 & 2 Sections) will be at the disposal of the attacking battalions.

(4) **Details of M.G. Barrage** Nos. 3 & 4 Sections will take up positions on Y/Z night at U.26.d.0.9 and U.26.a.9.2 respectively. Rapid fire (1 belt in 4 minutes) will be maintained from Zero to Zero + 40 mins on the following targets :-
No 3 Section CANIVES FARM to U.22.a.40.60.
No 4 Section U.22.a.45.65. to U.22.a.70.45.
At Zero + 40 mins. Both these sections will move forward to previously prepared positions 500 yds further forward, and from Zero + 1.40 to Zero + 3.10 will open fire on the following targets :-
No 3 Section U.16.d.5.9 to U.16.b.9.0
No 4 Section U.16.d.75.85 to U.17.a.2.1
(Rate of fire, intermittent bursts, except Zero + 2.40 to Zero + 3.10 at 1 belt in 4 mins.)

Notes (a) The following barrage positions will be dug and marked by red screens on Y/Z night. Six belts and two boxes of S.A.A. per gun will be taken there before Zero.
(b) A platform for the tripod must in all cases be sandbagged and made firm. Tripods must also be bedded in sandbags to prevent sinking. Lower limits of traverse must be blocked.
(c) Aiming posts giving all limits of arc & elevation for each gun, and one for each gun must be at the gun positions before Zero.
(d) Each gun will start the barrage with a new spare barrel, and a wet rag will be fired before gun barrels to cool. Barrels will be changed on completion of the night.

(c) Gun positions must be carefully checked by measurement as well as re-section.

(d) After Zero + 4.30 (3.10 9pm) all barrage guns will be ready to open fire in case of S.O.S. signal. Targets will be as for the barrage, but with an additional 200 yards range. Rate of fire 4 belts in first 4 minutes, then 1 belt in four minutes.

(5) **Rations.** Each man will carry three days' rations in addition to the emergency rations. Water bottles will be filled.

(6) **Strong Points.** Strong points will be constructed by battalions as follows:—
DETHAIN FARM, by 1st K.O.S.B
CANNES FARM, by 1st K.O.S.B
U.15. Central, by 2/ S.W.B
U.15.c.4.4., by 2/ S.W.B
CRAONNE FARM, by 2/ S.W.B

(7) **S.O.S. signal.** S.O.S. signal will be green lights fired from Very pistols.

(8) **Medical.** There will be dressing stations at RUISSEAU FARM and LAPIN FARM.

(9) **Dumps.** R.E. dumps are situated at STEAM MILL (B.6.d.3.2) and at C.6.0.3.9. S.A.A. dumps at PILS DUMP (C.1.c.1.9) DOODLES DUMP (B.6.b.9.5) and GREEN MILL (U.25.d.1.4) (The latter is also a water dump) There is also a battle dump at ABRI FARM. (U.26.a.3.2).

(10) Company H.Q. will be at U.26.c.25.30

(11) Acknowledge.

Issued at 1630

J.W.Moberly
Lieut & Adjt.
87th Machine Gun Company

Copies No 1. Office
" 2.) War Diary   Copies No. 11 86th M.G. Coy
" 3.)   12 227th M.G. Coy
4. O.C. No 1 Section
5. O.C. No 2 Section
6. O.C. No 3 Section
7. O.C. No 4 Section
8. 87th Infantry Brigade
9. D.M.G.O
10 86th M.G. Coy

SECRET

This Order to be attached to 6th M.G. Coy
Operation Order No. 18

I. Headquarters will be as follows at Zero:—

   87th Bde. Advanced H.Q. and report centre at SIGNAL FARM.
   Rear H.Q. at SAULES FARM.

   86th Bde. WOODHOUSE.

   2nd S.W.B. SENTIER FARM.

   1 K.O.S.B. CAPTAIN'S FARM, to move forward to PASSERELLE
   after Red Line has been taken.

   1 Border Regt. SIGNAL FARM, to move forward to WIJDENDRIFT
   after Red Line has been taken.

   A runner post will be established at CAPTAINS
   FARM and will be marked by a blue flag.

II. Nos. 1 & 2 Sections will send a runner back to Coy H.Q.
    as soon as possible after reaching objectives, giving their
    location and any other available information.

III. Runners will carry all messages in the top right breast
     pocket.

IV. A Field Ambulance relay post will be established
    at U.26.a.b.4 and at PASSERELLE FARM.

V. All communication will be by runners. One runner
   from No. 3 Sections and one runner from No. 4
   Section will report to Coy H.Q. before Zero.

Issued at 1900.

Copies 1 Office
       2-3 War Diary
       4-7 Section Officers

                                    J. Mobely
                                    Lt. [?]
                                    87 M.G. Coy

COPY

APPENDIX II

(1) XIV Corps Wire dated 17th. August 1917 is republished.

"Commander-in-Chief called on Corps"
"Commander this morning and ordered him to convey"
"his congratulations to all troops engaged in our"
"operations yesterday"

(2) From OC 1st. BORDER REGT:-

"The Officer Commanding 1st BORDER REGT."
"wishes to express his appreciation of the splendid"
"work performed by LIEUT. PAGE and the section of"
"your company under his command, who were"
"attached to this Unit for the action of 16th August"
"1917 near LANGEMARCK. They carried out his"
"instructions perfectly, in spite of the appalling nature"
"of the ground, and were of great assistance."

Vol 16

CONFIDENTIAL

"   "

WAR DIARY

OF
THE

87th MACHINE GUN COMPANY.

FROM 1st September 1917   To   30th September 1917.

(VOLUME XVI)

Army Form C. 2118.

WAR DIARY
or
INTELLIGENCE SUMMARY.
(Erase heading not required.)

Instructions regarding War Diaries and Intelligence Summaries are contained in F. S. Regs., Part II. and the Staff Manual respectively. Title pages will be prepared in manuscript.

Place	Date	Hour	Summary of Events and Information	Remarks and references to Appendices
In the Field	1st		Draft of 15 Other Ranks joined Company from Base	
	3rd		General Inspection and Presentation of Medals	
	4th		Lieut G.H. MOBERLY appointed Commanding Officer & Lieut H.G.M.C. RANDALL 2nd in Command	
	8th		Company marched to Training Area at HERZEELE for 4 days Training	
	11th		Lieut B. GREEN proceed to 191st Company	
	12th		Company returned from Training Area to PEGSWELL CAMP.	
	14th		1. O.R. Taken on Strength of Company from 86th Machine Gun Company	
	15th		1 O.R. Taken on Strength of Company from Base	
	18th		87th Brigade Group reviewed by General LA CAPELLE, commanding 1st French Corps. 87th Machine Gun Company took part, marching past with mules.	
			2. O.R. Evacuated Sick out of Divisional Area	
	20th		Company, with Transport marched to FOREST CAMP AREA, in Corps Reserve	
	25th		1 O.R. Evacuated Sick out of Divisional Area.	
	29th		Company proceeded to the line. — Nos 1 & 3 4 Sections relieved the 88th Machine Gun Company in the line LANGEMARCK Sector, No 2 Section and details remaining at Camp in EMILE FARM. Transport	

WAR DIARY
or
INTELLIGENCE SUMMARY.

(Erase heading not required.)

Army Form C. 2118.

Place	Date	Hour	Summary of Events and Information	Remarks and references to Appendices
In the Field	29th		Lines & Quarters Machine Stores remaining at Box Camp, FOREST Area.	
"	30th		1 O.R. Wounded in Action.	

A. Onward Lieut.
for O.C. 87th Machine Gun Coy

CONFIDENTIAL.

War Diary.

of the 87th Machine Gun Company.

From 1st October 1917 to 31st October 1917.

(VOLUME XVII)

Army Form C. 2118.

WAR DIARY
or
INTELLIGENCE SUMMARY.
(Erase heading not required.)

Instructions regarding War Diaries and Intelligence Summaries are contained in F. S. Regs., Part II. and the Staff Manual respectively. Title pages will be prepared in manuscript.

Place	Date	Hour	Summary of Events and Information	Remarks and references to Appendices
In the Field	2nd		No 2 Section relieved No 4 Section in the Centre Sector (LONGEMAR)	
	4th		No 3 Section, from positions at MONT MIRAIL F.M, fired a standing barrage in support of the advance of the 86th Brigade & the 1st K.O.S.B. The barrage was maintained from zero to zero + 7 (approx.)	
			Lieut C.H. PAYNE was wounded at zero, but remained at duty until noon.	
	5th		Company relieved by 3rd Guards Brigade M.G. Company & marched to COPPERNOLE CAMP (in Bivouacs)	
	8th		Company entrained at ELVERDINGHE 6 pm & detrained at PROVEN.	
	9th		Marched to PROVEN I Area & took over PILCH CAMP from 50th M.G. Regt.	
	10th		Lieut L. GORDON Taken on strength of Company from Base.	
			1 O.R. Evacuated sick out of Divisional Area	
	15th		Company with transport proceeded by road to PESELHOEK, where both Company & Transport entrained for THIRD ARMY AREA, at 6.30 p.m.	
	16th		Company & Transport detrained at SAULTY & marched to BELLACOURT	
	17th		Lieut H.G.M.C. RANDALL Taken on Strength of Company from U.K.	
	21st		1 O.R. Evacuated Sick out of Divisional Area	

Army Form C. 2118.

WAR DIARY
or
INTELLIGENCE SUMMARY.
(Erase heading not required.)

Instructions regarding War Diaries and Intelligence Summaries are contained in F. S. Regs., Part II, and the Staff Manual respectively. Title pages will be prepared in manuscript.

Place	Date	Hour	Summary of Events and Information	Remarks and references to Appendices
In the Field	25th		No 2 Section marched to MOYENNEVILLE & came under the orders of the 16th Division for the purpose of digging Gun positions	

P. Venturi Lieut.
for O Comm- 87th Machine Gun Company

CONFIDENTIAL.

WAR DIARY.
of the
87th Machine Gun Company
/29

From 1st November 1917 to 30th November 1917.

(VOLUME XVIII)

WAR DIARY
or
INTELLIGENCE SUMMARY.
(Erase heading not required.)

Army Form C. 2118.

Place	Date	Hour	Summary of Events and Information	Remarks and references to Appendices
BELLACOURT	1st		2 O.R. Evacuated to U.K. on Course of Instruction	
	5th		1 O.R. Evacuated Sick out of Divisional Area	
	7th		Lieut J GORDON Struck off Strength of Company (To Base)	
	8th		1 O.R. Joined Company from Base	
	10th		1 O.R. Evacuated Sick out of Divisional Area	
	13th		2 O.R. Taken on Strength of Company from Base	
	15th		1 O.R. Evacuated to U.K. On Course of Instruction.	
	16th		Transport proceeded by road to HAUT-ALLAINES.	
	17th		Company marched from BELLACOURT to entraining point (BOISLEUX-AU-MONT) detrained at PERONNE & marched to HAUT-ALLAINES	
HAUT-ALLAINES	18th		Company with Transport marched to FINS.	
FINS	19th		Company confined to camp all day to avoid been spotted by hostile aeroplanes. Company Operation Order No. 18 issued. (See Appendix $\frac{K}{1}$) At about 6.0 pm all pack mules were loaded & brought up to camp in readiness for move. N°s 1 & 4 Sections reported to 2nd S.W.B. & 1st R.O.S.B. respectively.	
	20th		Company (less Nos 1 & 4 Sections) moved from Camp to concentration area, which	

WAR DIARY
or
INTELLIGENCE SUMMARY.
(Erase heading not required.)

Army Form C. 2118.

Place	Date	Hour	Summary of Events and Information	Remarks and references to Appendices
In the Field	20th cont'd		was reached about 3.45 am. At 9.00 (6.20 am) the whole Brigade moved forward to our original front line captured the No. 2 & 3 Sections moving in rear of new Battalions. On completion of 4n 2nd objective by 6th, 20th and 12th Divisions, 87th Brigade advanced. No hostile shelling. No. 9 Sections advanced in file with mules. Nos 2 & 3 Sections taking up positions in L 34 central. At 3 pm the Sections were sent forward to front line on far side of Canal (about 500 yards short of final objective) & came under orders of 1st R. Inniskillings & came under hostile Machine Gun fire encountered. Respectively. Heavy hostile Machine Gun fire encountered. Owing to expected counter attacks & importance of maintaining Bridgeheads all guns except 6, went into front line, & being in close support & just behind the Canal guarding the back causeway. Reserve belt Boxes & S.A.A. were successfully got up before night. Very little Machine Gun fire done during attack owing to slight enemy resistance. No. 1 Section on the right supported 2nd S.W.B. crossing the Canal by direct overhead fire, be covering fire was necessary for capture of MARCOING. Casualties 5 O.R. Wounded.	

WAR DIARY
or
INTELLIGENCE SUMMARY.
(Erase heading not required.)

Army Form C. 2118.

Place	Date	Hour	Summary of Events and Information	Remarks and references to Appendices
MARCOING	21st		At noon, an advance was attempted to the RED LINE under cover of Tanks. Terrific enemy indirect machine gun barage was opened & attack failed. Direct overhead covering fire was given by No 3 Section to troops attempting to advance. Casualties: — 10 R. Killed	
	27th		Company relieved from front line by 88th Machine Gun Company. 10 Guns (No 3rd Section & 1 No 2 Section) proceeded to barage positions in G.32.a., covering right Brigade front. Remaining 6 Guns took up positions covering Canal crossings.	
	28th		Company took over front line again from 88th Machine Gun Company in Rifle Brigade Sector. One Other Rank taken on strength of Company.	
	30th		Heavy German counter attack took place at dawn on right flank. By 9.15 am Germans had reached a point about 800yds from MARCOING. One Machine Gun was taken from Canal defences and mounted on Brigade Headquarters (L.22.d.4.3.) This Gun fired on and helped to	

WAR DIARY
or
INTELLIGENCE SUMMARY.

Army Form C. 2118.

(Erase heading not required.)

Place	Date	Hour	Summary of Events and Information	Remarks and references to Appendices
MARCOING (contd)	March 30th (contd)		clock German advance. Meanwhile all spare gun numbers & all Company Headquarters manned the VILLERS-PLOUICH – MARCOING ROAD together with Brigade Headquarters, opening rapid rifle fire on enemy line. Enemy line thus checked, was finally thrown back by infantry counter attack. No guns of the Company except one, took part in these operations. As the attack came not from our own front but from our right rear, other guns manning our own front lines did not know the situation till evening. After dusk the whole of No. 1 Section (taken from Bridge Defences) and No. 3 Section (taken from our own support line) were swung round to protect our former right flank which now became part of our own front line. (L.30.a. – L.35.b.–R.5.a.)	

M. Nobely Capt.
Comm'dg 87th Machine Gun Coy.

SECRET   87th Machine Gun Company.   (APPENDIX I)
Operation Order No. 18.

Ref: Maps.   In the Field Nov: 1917
NIERGUIES, GOUZEAUCOURT combined Sheets 1/20,000.

1) On a date & at a zero hour to be notified later, an attack will be carried out by the III Corps, the attack on the 1st & 2nd Objectives (BLUE & BROWN LINES) respectively, being carried out by the 12th, 20th & 6th Divisions.
     The 29th Division will be in Corps Reserve & will be used for the capture of the 3rd Objective (RED LINE) after the Brown Line has been taken

2) The 87th Infantry Bde will attack MARCOING & will seize the Bridges over the Canal at L.23.b.1.8., L.23.a.7.0. and L.23.c.9.3. & will then push forward & capture the Red Line.

3) There will be no preliminary bombardment - but the attack on BLUE & BROWN Lines will be made under the protection of Tanks with the assistance of Standing Artillery & Smoke Barrages which will lift from objective to objective as the attack progresses

4) On Y/Z night the Brigade will be concentrated in Q.30.a, with Bde H.Q. at Q.29.d.2.9. At zero hour Bde will move up to the old front-line as follows:-
     2nd S.W.B. our front & support lines from SUNKEN Rd in R.8.d. (exclusive) to COPSE Rd in R.8.c., with 1st R. Innis Fus in gullies just behind
     1st KOSB our front & support lines from COPSE Rd in R.8.c. exclusive to R.7.b.9.0., with 1st Border Regt in gullies just behind
     Bde H.Q. will be at R.8.c.9.0.

5) As soon as the BROWN LINE has been captured the Bde will be ordered to move forward from our old front-line. General line of advance 40°/. true. The Signal for advance will be a "G" sounded on a bugle from Bde H.Q. which will be repeated by Battalions
     2nd S.W.B on Right and 1st KOSB on Left will form the front line. 1st R. Innis Fus on Right & 1st Border Regt on Left will form the Support Line.

6) Objectives.
     (a) 2nd SWB:- MARCOING COPSE & Canal Crossing at L.24.d.8.4.
     1st KOSB:- MARCOING & Canal Crossing at L.23.c.6.9. and L.23.b.1.8.
     These 2 Battalions will then, if the crossings are intact, each send 2 Companies across the Canal to form a

Bridgehead from the East of the Lock in L.24.c to the Lock in L.17.d.

(b) Directly the crossings have been captured 1st R. Innis. Fus + 1st Border Regt. will cross the Canal and supported by Tanks, will assault the RED LINE. This attack will take place whether the Tanks cross the Canal or not. On the capture of the Red Line, patrols will be pushed right forward and an outpost line established on the high ground in G.2. and G.3.

(c) When the Red Line is consolidated, 1st KOSB & 2nd SWB will advance & occupy the line G.2, G.3, RUMILLY.

7.) **Machine Gun Action**

(a) No.1 Section will be attached to & under the orders of O.C. 2nd SWB from Y day. 2 Guns will probably take up positions about L.30 to cover the Lock crossing in L.24. and 2 guns will probably go forward to the high ground in G.19. to protect the Bridgehead Line.

(b) No.4 Section will be attached to and under the orders of O.C. 1st KOSB from "Y" day. 2 Guns will probably take up positions about L.17.c. to cover the main Canal Bridge, & 2 guns will probably go forward to protect the Bridgehead Line

(c) Nos. 2 & 3 Sections will advance as soon as possible to the BROWN LINE about L.34 central from where they will be prepared to assist the attack on MARCOING by overhead covering fire. They will remain in these positions until they receive orders to move, when No. 2 Section will move up to the Red Line and report to O.C. 1st R. Innis Fus. and No. 3 Section will move up to the Red Line and report to O.C. 1st Border Regt.

(8) S.A.A. etc:—
Sections will take with them mules as follows:—
No. 1 Section 4 Gun mules & 3 Belt Box mules (24 Boxes)
No. 2   "   4   "   "   & 6   "   "   "   (48 Boxes)
No. 3   "   4   "   "   & 6   "   "   "   (48 Boxes)
No. 4   "   4   "   "   & 3   "   "   "   (24 Boxes)
Nos. 1 & 4 Sections will take mules as far as possible & will

then unload them & send them back to L.8.c.7.5 where they will wait till the Transport Officer meets them.

Nos 2 & 3 Sections will take their mules as far as possible & unloading only the Gun Mules. & 3 Belt Box Mules, they will make their own arrangements for getting all their mules forward.

When these Sections move forward all mules will be sent back to original forming up area before night. Transport Officer will move up to L.8.c.7.5 with 6 Belt Box Mules (& 8 Boxes) as soon as possible & form a dump there. He will meet there the 14 Mules of Nos 1 & 4 Sections and will send back 20 mules to the S.A.A. Dump at VILLERS PLOUICH to bring 40 Boxes S.A.A. to the dump at L.8.c.75. He will then arrange to send up 16 Belt Boxes & 10 Boxes S.A.A. to Nos 1 & 4 Sections.

If guides come back from these Sections they will be met at L.34. Centrl. In the absence of guides the Ammunition will be sent to L.23.c.2.3 and L.29.b.9.5 respectively.

9) Headquarters

Bde H.Q. will be first at Q.29.d.2.9 and then at L.8.c.8.0. On the capture of MARCOING it will move to L.34 Central and on the capture of the RED LINE it will move to MARCOING. Company H.Q. will be throughout with Brigade H.Q.

10) Counter Attacks

An Aeroplane will be up throughout the day whose sole mission will be to detect the approach of enemy counter attacks. It will signal an enemy counter attack by dropping a Smoke Bomb over the portion of the front at which the enemy is advancing. This smoke bomb will burst into a White Parachute flare leaving a brown trail of smoke behind it.

11) S.O.S. Signal will be a Rifle Grenade bursting into two Green & two ~~Red~~ White lights

12) Communications There will be a permanent Visual Station at L.34.d.5.7. when Bde H.Q. move to MARCOING

13) Medical

There will be a forward Advanced Dressing Station on the Road in R 5 b and also at GOUZECOURT. (Q.36.d.4.9.)
Regimental Aid Posts will allready have been established at R.20.d.7.4. and R.20.a.2.9.

As soon after zero as possible, Relay Posts will be established at L.28 b central — L.34.b.8.5. — L.36.a.5.0.

14) Markings of Tanks.

Tanks attached to 87th Bde will be marked as follows :-

 RED / GREEN

15) 1 Sandbag per man & 1 Pick & Shovel per team will be carried

16) Range Cards will be made on reaching a new gun position.

17) Water. Springs are reported at the following points L17.d.,60.95., — L.22.c 80.65. — L27.b.9.6.

18) Reports. — Reports will be sent back to Coy: H Q. as soon as possible after moving to a new Gun position

19) Acknowledge.

Issued at 1700

Copies

Nº 1 Office
2 & 3 War Diary
Nºs 4 - 7 Sections
8 — 87th Brigade
9 — DMGO
10 — 86th M G Coy.
11 — 88th M G Coy
12 — 227 M G Coy.
13 — Transport Officer

Lieut-
87th Machine Gun Coy

Vol 19

CONFIDENTIAL

WAR

DIARY

(VOLUME XIX)

87th MACHINE GUN COMPANY.
/29

From 1st December 1917 to 31st December 1917.

WAR DIARY or INTELLIGENCE SUMMARY

Army Form C. 2118.

Place	Date	Hour	Summary of Events and Information	Remarks and references to Appendices
In the Line	Dec. 1st		Owing to the Evacuation of MASNIERES by 86th Infantry Brigade, right flank of our line N. of Canal was drawn back and a new position taken up joining up with left of 2nd S.W.B. about R.19.d.1.7. No 2 Section 87th Machine Gun Company remained in original front line covering retirement of Infantry till they were safely back in new line. These four guns then rejoined Infantry. — 2 Guns taking up positions to cover the lock in L.24.c.	
"	2nd		Nos 2 & 4 Sections on N. bank of Canal were relieved by eight guns of 16th Machine Gun Company & proceeded to RIBECOURT in reserve.	
"	3rd		About 11 a.m. strong German bombardment commenced, followed by a general attack on 2nd S.W.B. front, (L.30.a.). No 1 Section attached to this Battalion fired on advancing Germans until 3 guns were blown up by shell fire. Only a few hundred yards of ground were lost on this front. Lieut. 6th Infantry Brigade were driven back on our left above the Canal, leaving MARCOING open to the enemy. Owing to the critical position this caused three machine guns were brought up from	

Army Form C. 2118.

WAR DIARY
or
INTELLIGENCE SUMMARY.
(Erase heading not required.)

Place	Date	Hour	Summary of Events and Information	Remarks and references to Appendices
In the Line	3rd		RIBECOURT into the HINDENBURG Support Line covering Valley about L.26.a. Also 3 guns in R.H.a were moved along the HINDENBURG Support line to L.33.a. covering the Railway & Valley leading to MARCOING.	
	4th		No further German attack developed. At 4:30 pm 108th Machine Gun Company took up positions in the line and remaining 7 guns of 87th Machine Gun Company evacuated their positions marching down to SOREL.	
SOREL	5th		Company less Transport entrained at 11:30 am at ETRICOURT & arrived at MONDICOURT about 6 pm. from here they marched to Billets at GRAND RULLECOURT. Transport proceeded by Road from SOREL via BAPAUME to GRAND RULLECOURT taking 2½ days to do the journey. Transport rejoined Company. 29th Division Special Order of the day received	
GRAND RULLECOURT	7th		1 O.R. joined Company from Base Depot.	(App I)

Army Form C. 2118.

WAR DIARY
or
INTELLIGENCE SUMMARY.

(Erase heading not required.)

Instructions regarding War Diaries and Intelligence Summaries are contained in F. S. Regs., Part II. and the Staff Manual respectively. Title pages will be prepared in manuscript.

Place	Date	Hour	Summary of Events and Information	Remarks and references to Appendices
GRAND RULLECOURT	9th		5 O.R. Evacuated Sick out of Divisional Area.	
	11th		2 O.R " " " " "	
			3 Officers Joined Company from Base Depôt (Lieut. E. GILDERTHORP, E.A. BOLTER, E. GODSON-BAX)	
	12th		1 Officer " " " " (2/Lt C. DARKE)	
			4 O.R. Evacuated Sick out of Divisional Area.	
	15th		1 O.R. " " " " "	
	17th		6 O.R Joined Company from Base Depôt. Company with Transport proceeded by march route to Billets in VACQUERIE stopping one night.	
VACQUERIE	18th		Company with Transport proceeded by march route to WAMIN. Billeted for one night.	
WAMIN	19th		Company with Transport proceeded by march route to Billets in HENCVILLE.	
HENCVILLE	20th		22 O.R Joined Company from Base Depôt.	
	21st		6 O.R Joined Company from Base Depôt. 4 O.R Evacuated Sick out of Divisional Area.	

Army Form C. 2118.

WAR DIARY
or
INTELLIGENCE SUMMARY.
(Erase heading not required.)

Instructions regarding War Diaries and Intelligence Summaries are contained in F. S. Regs., Part II. and the Staff Manual respectively. Title pages will be prepared in manuscript.

Place	Date	Hour	Summary of Events and Information	Remarks and references to Appendices
HENOVILLE	23rd	2 O.R.	Rejoined Company from Hospital	
	25th	1 O.R.	Transferred to 86th Machine Gun Coy. Reported to 87th M.G. Company in error.	
	31st	1 O.R.	To Machine Gun Base Depôt for transfer to U.K. on special course of instruction.	

J. Mosely
Capt.
Commdg: 87th Machine Gun Coy.

(APPENDIX I)

SPECIAL ORDER OF THE DAY
by
Major General Sir Beauvoir de Lisle, K.C.B., D.S.O.
Commanding 29th Division.

I wish to convey to the Troops of my Division my high appreciation of their gallant conduct and resolute determination during the operations from November 20th 1917 to the 4th December 1917, and to convey to all ranks the following messages which have been received by me:-

From Sir W.P. PULTENEY, K.C.B., K.C.M.G., D.S.O., Commanding III Corps.

"The Corps Commander would like to place on record his deep appreciation of the fighting spirit of the 29th Division. The magnificent defence of the MASNIERES-MARCOING line at a most critical juncture, and the subsequent orderly withdrawal reflects the highest credit on all concerned.
In the 15 days in which your Division has been in action on this front, all ranks have displayed an endurance which is beyond praise.
He would be glad if this could be conveyed to your troops."

From General Sir Julian BYNG, K.C.B., K.C.M.G., M.V.O. Commanding Third Army.

"I would like you to express to all ranks my sincere appreciation of the services which have been rendered to the Third Army by the 29th Division.
Both in the attack on the 20th November 1917 and in their defence of their sector on the 30th November 1917 and subsequent days, the Division has more than maintained its splendid reputation.
I ask you to accept my warmest congratulations."

From Field Marshal Sir Douglas HAIG, K.T., G.C.B., G.C.V.O., K.C.I.E. Commander-in-Chief British Armies in France.

"Please convey to General de Lisle and men of the 29th Division my warm congratulations on the splendid fight successfully maintained by them against repeated attacks by numerically superior forces. Their gallant defence of MASNIERES throughout two days of almost continuous fighting has had most important results upon the course of the Battle and is worthy of the best traditions of the British Army."

Beauvoir de Lisle

Major General,
Commanding 29th Division.

7th December 1917

SPECIAL ORDER OF THE DAY
by
Major General Sir Beauvoir de Lisle, K.C.B., D.S.O.
Commanding 29th Division.

I wish to convey to the Troops of my Division my high appreciation of their gallant conduct and resolute determination during the operations from November 20th 1917 to the 4th December 1917, and to convey to all ranks the following messages which have been received by me:-

From Sir W.P. PULTENEY, K.C.B., K.C.M.G., D.S.O., Commanding III Corps.

"The Corps Commander would like to place on record his deep appreciation of the fighting spirit of the 29th Division.
The magnificient defence of the MASNIERES-MARCOING Line at a most critical juncture, and the subsequent orderly withdrawal reflects the highest credit on all concerned.
In the 15 days in which your Division has been in action on this front, all ranks have displayed an endurance which is beyond praise.
He would be glad if this could be conveyed to your troops."

From General Sir Julian BYNG, K.C.B., K.C.M.G., M.V.O. Commanding Third Army.

"I would like you to express to all ranks my sincere appreciation of the services which have been rendered to the Third Army by the 29th Division.
Both in the attack on the 20th November 1917 and in their defence of their sector on the 30th November 1917 and subsequent days, the Division has more than maintained its splendid reputation.
I ask you to accept my warmest congratulations."

From Field Marshal Sir Douglas HAIG, K.T., G.C.B., G.C.V.O., K.C.I.E. Commander-in-Chief British Armies in France.

"Please convey to General de Lisle and men of the 29th Division my warm congratulations on the splendid fight successfully maintained by them against repeated attacks by numerically superior forces. Their gallant defence of MASNIERES throughout two days of almost continuous fighting has had most important results upon the course of the Battle and is worthy of the best traditions of the British Army."

Beauvoir de Lisle

Major General,
Commanding 29th Division.

7th December 1917

CONFIDENTIAL.

WAR DIARY

OF
THE

87th Machine Gun Company.

From 1st January 1918 to 31st January 1918.

(VOLUME XX)

WAR DIARY
or
INTELLIGENCE SUMMARY.

(Erase heading not required.)

Army Form C. 2118.

Instructions regarding War Diaries and Intelligence Summaries are contained in F. S. Regs., Part II. and the Staff Manual respectively. Title pages will be prepared in manuscript.

Place	Date	Hour	Summary of Events and Information	Remarks and references to Appendices
HENOVILLE	3rd		Company with Transport marched from HENOVILLE to billets in BORTHES for the night.	
BORTHES	4th		Company with Transport marched from BORTHES to billets in LAVAL D'ACQUIN.	
LA VAL D'ACQUIN	5th		2 OR Evacuated sick out of Divisional Area.	
	6th		do.	
	10th		1 OR to UK. for transfer to Officers Training Corps.	
	12th		1 OR Evacuated Sick out of Divisional Area.	
	15th		do.	
			1 MR	
	17th	1.30am	Company marched from LA VAL D'ACQUIN to entraining point, WIZERNES – Entraining at 7.0am, detraining at BRANDHOEK marched to Billets in VLAMERTINGHE, In Divisional Reserve.	
			Transport proceeded by road stopping the night at ZERMEZEELE.	
	18th		Transport proceeded to join Company at VLAMERTINGHE.	
VLAMERTINGHE	20th		Company with Transport marched to camp at BRANDHOEK evacuated by 88th M.G. Company.	
			2 OR Evacuated Sick out of Divisional Area.	
BRANDHOEK	31st		1 OR Evacuated Sick out of Divisional Area.	

Army Form 1118.

WAR DIARY
or
INTELLIGENCE SUMMARY.

(Erase heading not required.)

Instructions regarding War Diaries and Intelligence Summaries are contained in F. S. Regs., Part II. and the Staff Manual respectively. Title pages will be prepared in manuscript.

Place	Date	Hour	Summary of Events and Information	Remarks and references to Appendices
BRANDHOEK	25		Company Inspection in Brigade inspection by 2.O.b. Medals ribbons were given by 2.O.b. to the following:—	
			Capt. G.H. MOBERLY } M.C.	
			2/Lieut. J.P. ASHTON }	
			C/Q.M.S. FINLAY. S. — D.C.M.	
			12822 Pte HUTCHINSON }	
			65252 " BUTCHER. H } M.M.	
			57800 " McNIVEN. A. }	
			84449 " TERRETT. G. }	
28			Company with Transport moved to Camp at DEAD END, YPRES and became M.G. Company in Support.	

J. Moberly
Capt.